RENAISSANCE

RENAISSANCE

The Rebirth

of Liberty

in the Heart

of Europe

Václav Klaus

CATO INSTITUTE

Washington, D.C.

Library of Congress Cataloging-in-Publication Data

Klaus, Václav.
    Renaissance : the rebirth of liberty in the heart of Europe /
Václav Klaus
        p.   cm.
    Collection of 29 essays and speeches, 19 of which were published in
the author's Rebirth of a nation five years after (1994).
    Includes bibliographical references and index.
    ISBN 1-882577-47-7. — ISBN 1-882577-48-5 (pbk.)
    1. Czechoslovakia—Politics and government.—1989-1996.   2.Czech
Republic—Politics and government.   3. Czech Republic—Economic
conditions.   4. Czech Republic—Economic policy.   5. Klaus, Václav.
6. Politicians—Czech Republic—Biography.   I. Klaus, Václav. Rebirth of
a nation five years after.   II. Title.
DB2241.K57A5   1997
943.704' 3—dc21   97-18539
                                                                        CIP

Printed in the United States of America.

CATO INSTITUTE
1000 Massachusetts Ave., N.W.
Washington, D.C. 20001

If in the first attempt to create a world of free men we have failed, we must try again.

—F. A. Hayek
The Road to Serfdom

Contents

Foreword

Václav Klaus is, without a doubt, the most successful leader of a postcommunist nation in Europe. His leadership and vision have transformed what was among the most Stalinist states of the Warsaw bloc into the most bustling, vibrant, and open society in the region, in some ways surpassing even the long-established Western democracies neighboring it. His English-language speeches and essays, collected for the first time in this volume, offer unique insight into the process of transformation and are important not only for the historical record but for an accurate understanding of current events. They should be of interest to anyone who follows economic policy or foreign affairs generally, as well as anyone concerned with rolling back government powers and substituting a free society for state power.

A number of factors help to explain the remarkable success of the Czech transformation process. The long history of free society in Bohemia and Moravia; the unique Czech attitude toward authority, so well expressed in Jaroslav Hašek's great work *The Good Soldier Schweik*; and the relative lack of foreign indebtedness help to explain a great deal. Other factors may be more important, however, as Klaus explained in a lecture at the Cato Institute on December 4, 1995:

> In our country in the 1970s and 1980s, people like me were definitely on the other side of the barricade and had absolutely no chance to do anything in cooperation with the government. Such was not the case in other postcommunist countries. All our counterparts—in Hungary, in Poland—were members of various government and Communist party commissions on restructuring and reforming the system. They were involved deeply in that process, which not only is time-consuming but influences your thinking because you are engaged in trying to reform the system. We were never involved in such activities. We had no chance to be involved. Nobody asked us for advice, and therefore our thinking remained clear and straightforward. We never considered

reforming the communist society and economy. We knew
that they had to be rejected.

The very lack of experience in "reform communism" was an
advantage to those Czechs who sought authentic reform and the
return to a "normal society." A normal society required the systematic elimination of socialism and its replacement by civil society
and its attendant institutions of private property and freedom of
exchange, individual rights, and the rule of law.

While potential reformers in Hungary, Poland, Russia, and elsewhere were busily involved with high-level government reform
efforts, the future Czech reformers were arranging underground
seminars on the works of such classical liberal thinkers as Milton
Friedman and the Austrian-school economists F. A. Hayek and Ludwig von Mises. The former exerted a special influence on Klaus, as
he explains in his essay "The University of Chicago and I" in this
volume. The influence of Hayek and Mises was of a somewhat
different order; not only were they the foremost critics of socialism
in this century, but they hailed from neighboring Austria (Hayek's
name is of Czech origin) and provided a connection with an older
tradition of Czech liberalism that had been lost in the intervening
years of national socialist and communist tyranny. (I had the pleasure in 1989 of smuggling out of Prague one of eight existing carbon
copies of Tomás Ježek's translation of Hayek's *The Road to Serfdom*
and then smuggling 100 photocopies back from Vienna. Ježek and
Klaus were boyhood friends, and Ježek became the first minister of
privatization in the postcommunist government. Josef Zieleniec, an
economist who now serves as foreign minister of the Czech Republic,
was active in promoting the study of the works of Mises.) In the
interwar years of the first Czechoslovak republic, an earlier finance
minister, Karl English, drew on the wider tradition of Central European liberalism (including the Austrians) in an attempt to forge a
liberal, free-market, constitutional system.

When the first Civic Forum meetings were held in Prague at the
Magic Lantern Theater in 1989, the moral leadership of Václav Havel,
now president of the Czech Republic, was what most outside observers noted first. But also active from the beginning was the "other
Václav," Václav Klaus. Then an economist at the Institute of Forecasting of the Czechoslovak Academy of Sciences, Klaus emerged

quickly as an able organizer, a tough bargainer with the communist authorities, and a brilliant spokesman for the classical liberal alternative to socialism. He became the first noncommunist finance minister of Czechoslovakia since the communist takeover of the country and later prime minister of the Czech Republic in July 1992. In both capacities he guided the country through a systematic process of economic and legal transformation. After numerous political conflicts with the leadership of the autonomous Slovak republic, Klaus and his colleagues (notably Zieleniec) arranged what has come to be known as the "Velvet Divorce," one of the very few peaceful dissolutions of a state in modern European history.

Each of those episodes reveals Klaus's skills and moral leadership. Rather than endure endless bickering and hostility, Klaus proposed to the Slovak political leadership a peaceful divorce. The wisdom of that approach was not evident to everyone at the time, but subsequent events have shown the benefits of Klaus's proposal. Rather than lurch haphazardly into quasi-market reforms and "spontaneous privatization," Klaus insisted on the systematic recreation of the foundations of a free society and efficient market: clear property rights, an efficient system of contract, and the rule of law. In Poland and Hungary privatization was often carried out without clear legal rules, leading many investors—both foreign and domestic—to find to their regret that they did not have clear legal title to their "investments." In contrast, Klaus warned potential investors to wait until parliament and the lawyers had done the work of recreating appropriate legal rules.

With the expert advice and collaboration of a team of similarly minded economists, Klaus introduced one of the most remarkable and amazing privatization plans in modern history. The so-called voucher plan created both widespread public support for privatization and an efficient transfer of ownership rights from an irresponsible state to responsible private parties. Klaus insisted that the starting point of the reform was to take the socialist apologists at their word when they insisted that state industries and properties "belonged to the people." Thus, vouchers were offered for sale at a nominal price to all citizens of Czechoslovakia, and a system of auctions and bids was created in which properties were systematically transferred to private hands. The system was enormously successful and has been copied in other former communist countries. It took not only vision, as Klaus stresses in the essays in this book, but also great determination and fortitude to move a nation from socialist tyranny to liberty and a market economy.

This book gives a sense of the breadth of Klaus's interests and writing, covering subjects such as economic reform, ecological policy, the future of Europe, and the relationship between artistic endeavor and toleration. Although his academic training is in technical economics, Klaus reveals the breadth of interest and wry humor we associate with such Czech intellectuals as Václav Havel, Milan Kundera, and Jaroslav Hašek and offers penetrating insights into his subjects.

All of the essays and speeches in *Renaissance: The Rebirth of Liberty in the Heart of Europe* were originally written or delivered by Klaus in English, but they have been edited for standard American idiom and spelling, retaining their original flavor and expressive style but rendering them more accessible to American readers. Nineteen of the speeches and essays in this volume were first published in Prague by Ringier CR in 1994 under the title *Rebirth of a Nation Five Years After: Collection of Speeches of the Prime Minister of the Czech Republic.* They and the 10 additional speeches chart the evolution of the ideas behind the transformation of both the Federative Republic and the Czech Republic from communism to capitalism. Major themes recur and are amplified, which is why two speeches on the same topic (chapters 8 and 9), revealing changes in Klaus's thinking over a period of more than two years, are included.

The old saying about the challenge of undoing the catastrophe of socialism was that, while it's easy to turn an aquarium into fish soup, it's not so easy to turn fish soup into an aquarium. Klaus and his classical liberal colleagues in the Czech Republic have shown how a sophisticated knowledge of economics and of the legal, moral, and political foundations of a free society, when combined with an unwavering moral vision, can achieve what until recently was thought impossible. The speeches and essays in this volume help us to understand how this daunting task is being accomplished. They should also provide inspiration for citizens in contemporary welfare states—also faced with a task held by some to be hopeless—about how to begin to undo the disaster of welfare statism. The moral vision and the scientific understanding that Václav Klaus brings to bear on seemingly intractable problems are now available to the English-speaking world.

—Tom G. Palmer

Preface

This book discusses the unique experience of someone who has in the last seven years been deeply involved in the transformation of a formerly communist country into a free society based on political pluralism and a market economy. The transformation is not a short endeavor or an overnight change; it is a process that started at the moment of the political collapse of communism in 1989, that continues at varying speeds in different countries and regions of the world, and that will be with us for some time to come.

An outside observer would be able to write a systematic treatise about such a historic event, one of the crucial events of the 20th century, but an insider does not have enough time and peace to write such a book. Nevertheless, an authentic account of what happened and on what ideas and premises it was based is necessary, or at least useful. We should not wait for retirement or a political failure. This book contains, therefore, speeches and other texts written for various occasions abroad. Their original language is English; there are no Czech versions of most of them. Invitations to make speeches, to open conferences, to receive awards and honorary degrees motivated me to explain different aspects of the transformation process, its difficult details as well as its positive results.

I would like to express my gratitude to all who helped with suggestions and criticism, to those in my office who spent hours typing and repeatedly correcting the original texts, and especially to Tom Palmer and Elizabeth W. Kaplan of the Cato Institute for making the publication of this book possible.

PART I

THE PROCESS OF TRANSFORMATION

1. Rebirth of a Region: Central Europe Five Years after the Fall

As you probably know, this evening is a very special one for this country. It was just five years ago that our students organized their famous demonstration not more than several hundred meters from this spot. The demonstration started the Velvet Revolution that brought about the collapse of communism in this country. I spent the last two hours with students of the Philosophical Faculty of Charles University in Prague, and the meeting was really very refreshing. It gave me a good chance to think about all that has happened, and I would like to continue in the same spirit now.

I must confess that I remember that evening five years ago quite clearly. I was coming from the railway station after a trip abroad, and in front of our house I met my elder son, who was coming back from the students' demonstration. He was shocked, he was scared, he was trembling. He told me what had happened, describing the peaceful nature of the students' demonstration and the unexpected and incredible police brutality. He terminated his story with the following statement: "We children did what we could; now it is the task of the parents to take over."

I hope that by taking over the torch we have succeeded in changing the country from communism to a free society with a market economy—no more, no less. I am deeply convinced that the results are unexpectedly good. I am aware that the achievements are different in different countries of the region, and I hope that they are better in this country than anywhere else, but the whole region has changed, and I disagree with occasional high-brow, detached, categorical, and unfounded statements that our success is below expectations. I have to argue that those commentators were either wrong 10 years ago when they thought communism was the embodiment

Speech delivered at the Atlantic CEO Institute Conference, Palais Wallenstein, Prague, November 1994.

of evil, the most undemocratic and inefficient system, or they are wrong now when they argue that it should have been possible to overcome the legacy of communism in as short a period of time as they might have wished and in a way they would have liked to impose upon us.

The ongoing transformation process has two sides from the point of view of policy—one rather passive, the other active. Both of them are very radical and revolutionary; both are based on a clear and transparent vision of the future, on the ability to sell that vision to the citizens of the country, and on a pragmatic but rational (definitely not simple) transformation strategy. The distinction between those two sides is important to an understanding of the logic of the whole process.

The passive (nonconstructivist and noninterventionist) side is identified with deregulation and liberalization. The political trans-formation was fully based on liberalization, on creating precondi-tions for free entry into the political market. We understood very early on that liberalization was sufficient and that no direct measures were necessary (it was not necessary to prohibit anything). That is a nontrivial conclusion. The free space was very rapidly filled with new political entities and now, in this country at least, a standard political structure—based on ideologically well defined political par-ties—has already been developed.

The economic transformation was, of course, based on liberaliza-tion as well. It has been proved that deregulation of markets— that is, of prices, foreign trade, and private entrepreneurship—is necessary for a fundamental change of the system, but we realized that it was not sufficient. A passive transformation would last too long and would be too costly. It was, therefore, supplemented with active transformation measures. I do not intend to discuss them in detail here; I will only outline their basic structure. It is helpful to use standard economic terminology and divide the measures into microeconomic and macroeconomic.

The most important change at the microeconomic level was gen-eral privatization. In our country we managed to effect the fastest and most extensive transfer of property rights to individuals. As you know, it is much easier to nationalize than to privatize; it is more difficult to build than to destroy. It took a very special mix of standard and nonstandard privatization methods, and the innova-tive Czech privatization by voucher proved to be a catalyst for the whole process. Now, five years after the Velvet Revolution and four years after the beginning of privatization, massive privatization is practically over. We have to solve some residual problems, as does any Western country, but that is part of our post-transformation task and challenge.

At the macroeconomic level, the task was to end the paternalism of the state, eliminate all forms of subsidies, keep the state budget in balance, and pursue an independent monetary policy. All that has been done. Using my standard analogy and describing the three consecutive transformation stages as waiting in a hospital ward, undergoing surgery, and recovering in a rehabilitation center, I can assure you that we have made it to the rehabilitation center. And we are in pretty good shape now.

Nothing else is necessary. Some people, here and elsewhere, would like to take advantage of the end of communism to create something more than a free society. They protested against our visions and strategies five years ago; they continue to protest now. They would like to have, not only free men and women, but better men and women as well. And they believe they know how to do it, how to "better" us; they know what is wrong with all of us and why. We are too materialistic, too selfish, too short-sighted, too self-centered; we consume more dumplings and meat than books and CDs of classical music. They don't consider liberalization sufficient. They want to transform not only institutions and rules but people as well.

I agree with attributing positive signs to such values, but I disagree with people who aspire to impose them upon us. Violation of human nature as a byproduct of collectivist ambitions resulted in an Orwellian totalitarian system, and we are happy it is over. Violation of human nature to fulfill moralist, elitist, and perfectionist ambitions would result in a Huxleyan Brave New World, which would lead us to new complications. We have to continue our struggle for a free society, and I am sure we will prevail.

2. The Interplay of Political and Economic Reform Measures in the Transformation of Postcommunist Countries

The worldwide breakdown of communism at the end of the 1980s gave us a unique, we may say an epochal, opportunity to get rid of the irrationalities and injustices of the old, discredited communist regime and to build on its ruins a standard system of political pluralism and democracy and an unconstrained market economy. The country I represent here tonight, the Czech Republic, is in that respect no exception. If there is anything special about my country, anything I should—with unhidden pride and satisfaction—stress here, it is its very fast progress in both the political and the economic components of the transformation process. I believe that the Czech Republic has already crossed the Rubicon dividing the old and the new regimes. That is an important achievement; we may become proof that the transformation from communism to a free society can be realized.

The topic of my lecture, and the object of my curiosity, is the reasons for the visible and irrefutable differences in the speed as well as the nature of the transformation process in various postcommunist countries. I will draw on my experience to outline some of the underlying principles of an optimal reform strategy for all countries that may find themselves facing a challenge similar to the one my country faced.

Even without a detailed and profound analysis, it is apparent that there are postcommunist countries that have had very modest success, countries that have fallen into what I call the reform trap—the vicious

Speech delivered at the Heritage Foundation in Washington, D.C., October 1993, and upon receipt of an honorary doctorate from the University of Francisco Marroquin, Guatemala, October 1993.

circle of incomplete and incorrect reform measures, of increasing inflation and unemployment, of public budget deficits and foreign indebtedness, of accelerating political troubles, of myopic policies that generate even worse outcomes, of chaos and anarchy. We know that such a circle usually ends in a deep politicoeconomic crisis and in the undermining of chances for future success.

There are, however, countries that have avoided falling into the reform trap, countries that have been able to initiate a virtuous circle based on a mixture of reasonable and therefore effective reform measures. Such a circle brings about positive economic results, political stability, and continuation of reforms.

The huge differences we witness are, in my opinion, the result of a specific interplay of political and economic factors in the transformation process. Those factors support and complement each other. To me, the central role of the interplay between economic policies and the political environment is self-evident, but it is often forgotten, or at least not fully appreciated.

Systemic transformation is not an exercise in applied economics or in applied political science. It is a process that involves human beings; that affects their day-to-day lives; that creates new groups of gainers and losers; that changes the relative political and economic strength and standing of different socioeconomic groups; and that thereby destroys the original political, social, and economic equilibrium. The communist system was characterized by its own peculiar, relatively stable equilibrium. Whether the new equilibrium—and especially the path from one equilibrium to another—is stable or unstable depends on the aforementioned interplay. I can draw the following lessons from our experience.

Vision

To be successful, political leaders must formulate and "sell" to the citizens of the country a positive vision of a future society.

The first task is formulation of the vision; it must be positive (not just negative); it must be straightforward (not fuzzy); it must motivate; it must speak to the hearts of men and women who have spent most of their lives under a spiritually empty communist regime. It requires clear words, biblical yeses and nos; it must be stated in an ideal form (which needs "extreme" terms, because compromises belong to reality, not to images or visions); it must explicitly reject all "third ways," which are based on incompatible combinations of different worlds.

The communist regime demonstrated, and we have fully understood, that human nature does not want Brave New Worlds (to use Aldous Huxley's apt term) and that to construct a free and functioning social system on dreams, on moral imperatives, or on somebody else's preferences is absolutely impossible. We accept Adam Smith's teaching—his vision of a free, democratic, and efficient society in which the citizen, not an enlightened monarch or an elitist intellectual, is king. Because of that, fulfilling the first task—formulating a vision—is not difficult. It just requires knowing and following proven, time-honored principles.

The second task, selling the vision, is much more complicated. It requires us to address the people, to argue, to explain, to defend; it requires permanent campaigning. It requires more than a good communications system, more than sophisticated information technology, more than free and independent mass media. It requires the formation of standard political parties because without them the politicians have no real power base and there is no mechanism for democratically creating policies, ideologies, and visions. Most postcommunist countries started the transformation without established political parties (and without positive visions) and were, therefore, unable to establish a basic, sufficiently strong pro-reform consensus and to start introducing necessary reform steps.

The political and social cohesion of a country cannot be cultivated without the permanent interaction of political parties. That is something to which the citizens (and politicians) in postcommunist countries were not accustomed. Overcoming distrust of political parties is not easy, but it must be done as soon as possible.

Changes

The necessary reform steps include both changes of institutions and changes of behavioral and regulatory rules—the rules of the game.

Without profound institutional changes, we cannot establish new agents in the game: citizens, political parties, parliaments, and small constitutionally constrained governments in the political sphere; consumers, suppliers of labor, firms, and independent central banks in the economic sphere (to name the most important ones). Those changes create a totally new institutional or organizational structure for the whole society.

Rules are changed by new, spontaneously created habits and customs as well as by new legislation and subsequent policies. The substance of legislation and policies is on the one hand to deregulate and liberalize and on the other to define principal constraints on and limits to the decisionmaking spaces for participating agents. That is the only way to unlock markets, to unleash private initiative, to eliminate excessive state interference, to let the new agents behave in a rational way.

Institutional changes take time. Changes of rules, however, can and must be made very fast. Much of the disagreement about the speed of transformation (shock therapy or gradualism) can be resolved if a proper distinction is made between the speed of those two conceptually different transformation tasks.

Blueprints for Reform

Such a fundamental change of an entire society cannot be dictated by a priori, preplanned, or prearranged procedures. Reform blueprints must be loose, unpretentious, and flexible. The dreams of social engineers of all ideological colors—dreams of organizing or masterminding the whole process of a systemic transformation in a rigid way—are false, misleading, and dangerous. It must be accepted as an important transformation theorem that it is impossible to centrally plan the origin and rise of a free society and a market economy.

The reformers must accept that the process involves not just them but millions of human beings with their own dreams, preferences, and priorities. The role of politicians in it must, therefore, be rather limited. They can guide and inspire, introduce necessary legislation, implement appropriate policies; they should not, however, try to dictate, command, or order. Democracy is indispensable, and attempts to ignore it in the name of easier and faster reform are futile and ineffective.

The Nature of Reform

Reform must be bold, courageous, determined, and, therefore, painful, because

- economic activities based on subsidized prices, on artificial demand (formerly created by fiat and now nonexistent), and on sheltered markets must cease to exist;
- a one-time price jump after price deregulation is unavoidable;
- drastic devaluation, which must occur before liberalization of foreign trade, shifts the exchange rate very far below purchasing power parity;
- disparities in income and property grow to an unprecedented level.

Those changes and their impacts must be announced and explained ahead of time, vigorously defended, and "survived." The costs the people have to bear must be widely shared; otherwise their fragile political support is lost. Telling the truth, not promising things that cannot be realized, and guarding the credibility of reform programs and of the politicians who realize them are absolute imperatives.

One-time changes are necessary byproducts of any kind of systemic transformation; galloping inflation or hyperinflation, repeated devaluations, prolonged declines in gross domestic product, state budget deficits, and growing foreign indebtedness are, however, avoidable by a positive interplay of political and economic reforms and by the introduction and implementation of rational macroeconomic policies based on conservative foundations.

Monetarism, not Keynesianism; fixed rules, not fine-tuning; a balanced budget, not fiscal activism; self-reliance, not dependence on foreign mercenaries—those are inspiring words for all of us who want to accomplish a historic transformation, for all of us who want to create a free, democratic, and efficient society.

3. The Ends and the Beginnings: University Studies and Systemic Change

It is a great honor and a great pleasure to have the opportunity to share some of my views with you—the views of one coming from a small Central European country, a country that in the last decades lived through a very frustrating communist experiment, a country that in the last few years has been realizing a most radical transformation of the whole social system. I come here as the prime minister of a foreign, yet friendly, country whose people see your country as the most important and most reliable guarantor of freedom, democracy, international stability, and security in today's world.

There is no doubt that this impressive and exciting commencement ceremony is for you the end of something, the end of several years of difficult studies, and at the same time the beginning of something, the beginning of an adult, mature, and in many respects more complicated or more responsible life. That simultaneity reminds me of another example of ends and beginnings. In my country, and in my part of the world, we have witnessed (and enjoyed) the end of communism and the beginning of a new era, the beginning of a free society.

Let me say a few words about that crucial turning point in the history of mankind and its implications for all of us in the postcommunist world as well as your country and elsewhere. When discussing the end of communism, I feel obliged to warn against simplistic approaches and interpretations and against unfounded expectations that, paradoxically, would lead us in the wrong direction.

Communism was an immense human tragedy, but it should be neither demonized nor underestimated. Demonization implicitly

---

Commencement address delivered at the Fletcher School of Law and Diplomacy, Tufts University, Boston, May 1994.

suggests that communism was a unique, unrepeatable event, something that fell from somewhere upon its innocent victims without their guilt, without their tacit approval or active cooperation. That is not true. Communism is only an extreme form of statism, of human constructivism, of political and social engineering. It is a system in which somebody knows better than the rest of society what is good for us, in which one and only one interpretation of freedom, justice, social equality, or economic rationality is declared to be obligatory. Communism is a world of extreme bureaucratism, of too many directives and prohibitions, of oppression and human degradation, of citizens who are powerless vis-à-vis the omnipotent state.

I dare to argue here today that a milder form of all that exists in a typical Western society, where it has its history of ups and downs, where it has, as well, its unpleasant internal dynamics that can suddenly reach the point at which the whole society slides into an unplanned, unintended state of affairs. To study our experience is, therefore, extremely important for Western countries.

I am a witness—both at home and abroad—to the trivialization of our situation. It is manifested in many ways, especially in continuing surprise that we have not yet solved all our inherited problems. Recently, after his return from my country, one influential American businessman announced publicly—with undisguised disappointment—that it is still easier to do business with Western Europe. I have to argue that communism would not have been so evil, so harmful, so extremely inefficient and irrational had it been possible to overcome its heritage in such a historically short time.

I am sure you know how long social phenomena take. For us in the postcommunist world, transformation is not a homework assignment or an exercise in applied economics or applied sociology or political science; our transformation is not done in a vacuum; the players in this radical societal change are not passive objects but human beings with their own dreams, habits, preferences, and priorities. You study the dynamics of that trivial (as compared to our systemic change) phenomenon called the business cycle; you know that its ups and downs cannot be avoided and that even their timing is unpleasantly resistant to all attempts of your politicians to influence them before or after elections.

I can afford to argue that the Czech Republic is undergoing the fastest and most successful systemic change in the whole postcommunist world: We have already created a standard system of ideologically well defined political parties. We have succeeded in achieving and maintaining a basic political and social consensus about the transformation vision, strategy, and results. We have introduced a market economy, based on massive and unprecedented privatization, deregulation, and liberalization, as well as a high degree of macroeconomic stability.

There is, however, no automatic transition between communism and a free society; between a command economy and a market economy; between a closed, compartmentalized society and an open, coherent society. It is a total misunderstanding to expect that after the end of one system, a new system will begin to function efficiently the next day, as if nothing had happened.

Moving from one system to another is a unique complex of intended measures and unintended events. That uncontrollable mixture of intentions and spontaneity is something other than constructivist dreams about optimal sequencing of reform measures, described in sophisticated scientific journals. When I saw a critical remark in the *Wall Street Journal* recently that the gross domestic product of the Czech Republic was still stagnant in 1993, I had to remind everyone that in a systemic change we are talking about qualities, not quantities, that we are opening markets, not maximizing GDP growth in the last quarter. Reading newspapers and watching TV, you can see that individual postcommunist countries have reached different transformation stages.

We in our country accepted an unconstrained vision, a vision of a society based on human action, not on human design (to use the powerful terminology of Friedrich von Hayek and Adam Ferguson). Nevertheless, creating such a system requires that the government play a positive and constructive role. The reformers have to dismantle the old institutions, and the resulting institutional vacuum must soon be filled with an alternative coordinating mechanism. Otherwise, the new system will not work. The faster the restructuring and market widening and deepening, the lower the economic and social costs and the more successful the whole systemic change.

I am not here to talk about our domestic problems and our ways of solving them. I want to turn your attention to the fragility of the political, social, and economic system, which we take for granted all too often. I want to warn against an unfounded belief in the disappearance of conflicts of visions. One conflict may be over, but conflicts of perhaps a more subtle nature are here. I disagree with the idea that the world has gotten to a stage called the end of history or the end of ideology. That is not true, will never be true. As long as human beings are human beings, there will be ideological conflicts. The conflict between communism and free society dominated the world in the past decades, but today's conflicts are no less important. We are—after decades of communism—oversensitive in this respect and see it as our duty to warn against the invisible or insufficiently visible potential dangers.

Today's world again faces the fundamental dispute between faith in the unconstrained interplay of free citizens and faith in the delegation of power to benevolent politicians and administrators, between faith in free trade and faith in fair trade (which means protectionism), between free markets and government industrial policies, between free choice based on our individual preferences and a priori external standards.

The so-called social dumping issue is a typical example of the new conflict of visions. It is suggested to us with all sincerity that free trade is fair only when foreign traders meet certain, externally formulated, "standards." The whole idea is based on the morally strange and intellectually untenable argument that different labor costs across firms or countries represent a "distortion of competition" and that such a deficiency must be remedied by enlightened supranational regulation. The claims for quasi-universal social rights are disguised attempts to protect high-cost producers in highly regulated countries, with unsustainable welfare standards, against cheaper labor in less productive countries. The gap between North and East or South does not stem from differences in regulations or social legislation; it is a direct reflection of a massive productivity gap. The postcommunist and developing countries cannot raise wages above productivity, and no international conferences or gatherings can help them to increase their productivity. Their unemployment rates and general poverty can, however, go up if external standards are imposed upon them.

The conflict of visions is here to stay, and we have to talk about it. I hope free speech will never be swapped for fair speech because fairness would be dictated by well-intentioned advocates of one or another indisputable truth.

4. Systemic Change: The Delicate Mixture of Intentions and Spontaneity

I do not intend to present a more or less standard, descriptive summary of the current stage of the transformation process in my country and elsewhere in Central and Eastern Europe. I find it appropriate to defend the results achieved thus far because, in spite of all existing problems, this historic transformation process has been, in principle, successful. Nevertheless, it is our task to understand more deeply the fascinating social mechanism that makes such a process possible and to describe the delicate interplay of its political, social, and economic factors.

My theoretical background and my practical experience tell me that systemic change—which we have been undergoing while dismantling communism in our countries—is an evolutionary process and not an exercise in applied economics or political science. It is based on a very complicated mixture of planned and unplanned, of intended and unintended, events, or, to put it differently, on a mixture of intentions and spontaneity. By participating in that process, we have opened another chapter in the never-completed book devoted to the study of the relative roles of human action and human design in the history of mankind, to the study of "made orders" and "catallaxies," to use the well-known Hayekian terms. I hope we can add something to that study. We may confirm that successful transformation is the result, not of detailed reform blueprints in the hands of omnipotent reform politicians, but of the unconstrained activity of millions of human beings together with "modest constructivism" in regard to foundational rules and the ability of

---

Address delivered to the general meeting of the Mont Pèlerin Society, Cannes, France, September 26, 1994. Earlier versions of this address were presented at the Centro de Estudios Publicos, Santiago de Chile, and at the Instituto Liberal, Rio de Janeiro, in April 1994. A slightly different edited version appeared in *Cato Journal* 14, no. 2 (Fall 1994): 171–77.

political leaders to implement the right transformation policies; those conditions are absolutely sufficient.

I believe that a negative stance toward ambitious constructivism and toward all forms of regimentation of free citizens is essential for all of us. We have learned that this idea is as relevant for the explanation of changes inside an existing system as for that of the transition from one social system to another. Again and again we in transforming countries have to caution against attempts to follow scientifically prepared sequencing rules for restructuring and constructing political, social, and economic institutions.

Our ability to control social events is restricted, and we know that no masterminding of reform (or transition) measures is possible. I stress that impossibility because we are traditionally a priori against all forms of political constructivism and social engineering, and in addition we have learned from experience that they are unrealizable in practice. While assisting in the creation of a new social order, we have to implement liberalization and deregulation measures (which is a more or less passive contribution). However, we also have to prepare and enact new rules that define certain abstract features of the new order (which is a more active contribution). Ultimately, we have to accept the existence of an evolutionary, spontaneous process, which finally establishes new political, social, and economic arrangements.

The question is whether and how those mechanisms should interact and how the spontaneous side should be supplemented by reason, by intended measures aimed at avoiding chaos and heavy transformation costs. By raising this question, I definitely do not mean to defend utopian social constructivism. Nevertheless, the intended, organized measures are important because the transition has its internal logic, and an understanding of that logic makes the process shorter and diminishes transformation costs.

Systemic change, which usually starts unexpectedly in a sudden outburst of popular discontent, is a complicated mixture of intentions and spontaneity. It seems to me that the transformation process has three stages and that each stage has a spontaneous and an intentional side.

Stage 1

Spontaneous Side

The whole process starts with the collapse of old institutions and rules. They are either swept away or become irrelevant. To achieve that result in the last days of communism was relatively simple, and the danger was not the possibility of return but the initiation of a vicious circle of half measures and truncated evolutionary changes leading to no improvement in either the moral or the efficiency properties of the new order. This moment presents the first crucial transformation danger. A long chaotic process or a more or less controlled and fast formation of a new, coherent system are the two potential alternatives.

Politically, the ruling communist party ceases to govern (and sometimes even to exist). A simple and very favorable political situation—a temporary nationwide unity—is achieved. That unity, however, exists only in a negative sense (dislike of the old system).

A unique and unrepeatable psychological euphoria prevails. There is a widespread readiness to actively participate in reversing the past; in getting rid of old, unpopular institutions; and even in "tightening belts." That moment is suitable for fast implementation of various painful and unpopular measures.

Economically, central planning (I use this term with some reluctance because nothing like the textbook central planning ever existed in our country) disappears practically overnight and with it the old, extremely inefficient, but nevertheless feasible, economic coordinating mechanism. An institutional vacuum is created. Very weak and heavily constrained, mostly implicit markets start to function; but without formal deregulation, without their opening by price liberalization, and without widespread implementation of explicit property rights, they cannot function efficiently. At that moment somebody has to react and to implement a coherent set of system-changing measures.

Intentional Side

Politically, we understood that no direct measures against the communist party were necessary or even helpful. It is sufficient to liberalize the political environment—that is, to ensure free entry for emerging political parties. As a result, the basically unreformed communist party remains a political entity, but unimportant and in opposition. If the original communist party is forbidden, the communists in renamed parties succeed in controlling the parliament afterwards, as they have in Poland and Hungary.

New political parties are spontaneously created, begin to formulate positive visions of the future, and try to explain them to the citizens of the country. That is the only way to transform the national unity (and consensus) from a negative to a positive one.

In the economic sphere, termination of the existing economic paternalism—a radical, bold, but "nonconstructive," measure—is crucial. Swift elimination of subsidies of all kinds, which brings about a dramatic upward shift in prices, must be undertaken without hesitation. Later on it becomes difficult or impossible to do that because newly formed pressure groups successfully block it. The authorities have to resist pleas for "constructive" supplementary measures—for helping firms in trouble by picking future winners and losers. Such a dramatic move changes the whole climate of the country. Goods, services, and all kinds of economic assets suddenly acquire their true values, and people are confronted with them. In this process there is no room for any form of gradualism, and this specific measure must be implemented in a "shock-therapy" manner. The result is the emergence of a totally different way of thinking, which is exactly what is necessary for changing old behavior and breaking old habits. There is no alternative. No "teaching" can lead to new behavior. It can be brought about only as a result of sheer necessity.

Together with the elimination of subsidies, macroeconomic stabilization, as a precondition for liberalization and deregulation of markets, must be initiated. After decades of grave economic disequilibria at both the macro- and the microlevel, fiscal and monetary policies must be very restrictive. Otherwise, rapid inflation starts to dominate economic and social life, blocking further reforms and jeopardizing the fragile social peace. A state budgetary surplus (or at least a balanced budget) and a very cautious monetary policy (a slower rate of growth of money supply than of nominal GDP) are indispensable. Public finances must be "firmly" in the government's hands. The central bank must be, on the contrary, fully independent. Without such preparatory steps, price and foreign trade liberalization measures represent an irresponsible move that solves nothing but aggravates existing economic difficulties and makes other reform measures impossible to implement.

Liberalization steps cannot wait. Opening of domestic markets (by means of price liberalization) and of foreign markets (by means of foreign trade liberalization) must follow the previous two steps. Without liberalization, economic agents cannot behave rationally, government cannot step out of economic intervention, and a new coordinating mechanism cannot be efficient. Liberalization should be accompanied by internal convertibility of the currency, and our experience tells us that for a small open economy it is extremely helpful when the exchange rate is fixed and becomes the nominal anchor of the whole economy, the only fixed variable in the system. (Alternative nominal anchors are less reliable and more difficult to maintain.)[1]

To summarize, the main tasks of the first stage include political liberalization, elimination of old subsidies, fiscal and monetary stabilization policies, independence of the central bank, a balanced budget, and liberalization of prices and foreign trade.

Stage 2

Spontaneous Reaction to Liberalization and Deregulation

The expectations of the citizens are enormous at this stage, yet positive, tangible results are not yet to be seen. After decades of zero inflation, zero unemployment, slow, distorted, but undeniable economic growth, relatively simple and undemanding life, the non-zero transformation costs must be paid. Inflation and unemployment appear (their magnitude depends, however, on the success or failure of previous reform steps), and a dramatic decline in GDP and in living standards becomes inevitable. It is difficult to explain to the public that we are not going through an economic crisis or recession caused by macroeconomic mismanagement but through a healthy transformation shakeout of nonviable economic activities.

As a result of the high and unpleasant transformation costs, the former euphoria "evaporates." The nationwide unity (which was mostly negative) is lost, and the scene is gradually dominated by conflicting positive visions of the future. That results in an enormous degree of political atomization and in increasing political instability.

New pressure groups are formed, and they begin to misuse the existing institutional vacuum, the weak markets as well as various

[1]For other arguments in favor of a fixed exchange rate regime, see Václav Klaus, "The Macroeconomic Aspect of Systemic Change: A Lesson Drawn from the Czech Experience," *Prague Economic Papers* 2, 1994; and Don Patinkin, "Israel's Stabilization Program of 1985, Or Some Simple Truths of Monetary Policy," *Journal of Economic Perspectives* 7, no. 2 (Spring 1993): 103–28.

gaps and holes in rapidly changing legislation and in the initiated privatization process (especially during the "spontaneous" privatization of state firms). Disparities in wealth and income grow, markets remain imperfect, and privatization revolutionizes the whole social structure.

At that moment comes the second turning point: either the original transformation strategy is adhered to with consequent positive results, or chaos and a vicious circle of half measures and concessions to pressure groups is initiated, with the inevitable loss of "the whole."

Intentional "Fixing Up"

The rules of the new order must be stabilized, and new legislation should redefine the rules of the game. The politicians should resist the temptation to rule by means of laws instead of making laws solely for defining the rules of the game.

Macroeconomic stabilization must continue. There is absolutely no room for expansionary monetary policy or for fiscal activism. Disinflation must go further, and a fixed exchange rate should be maintained.

New market distortions need not be created; the residual deregulation of prices, the elimination of remaining subsidies, and the aggressive fight against all forms of protectionism should not decelerate. No concessions to vocal pressure groups should be made.

New private firms spontaneously emerge, but organized privatization, done by a mixture of standard and nonstandard methods, represents the core of the intentional part of stage 2. Privatization of a whole country has a different scope, style, and meaning than does privatization in a country where it is only a marginal activity. Countrywide privatization must be fast, it must discover new owners, it should not attempt to maximize state privatization revenues, and it should not be confused with restructuring (and modernizing) individual firms (see chapter 12).

Politicians must offer clear rules and be accountable. No false promises should be made, and there must be a permanent explanatory campaign with the objective of maintaining or even strengthening the fragile political and social consensus. Without it, the transformation process cannot continue.

Standard political parties (instead of civic initiatives, national fronts, and civic forums) start to prevail. The extreme political atomization is slowly transformed into a normal political structure with only a handful of ideologically well defined political parties.

Reasonable social policy—concentrated on helping those who really need it—must accompany the political and economic changes. Wrongly targeted, extremely costly welfare programs should be avoided—a social "spotlight" approach should replace the social "sun" approach. Social policy must be formulated with due respect for those social groups that are the short-term losers in the transformation process.

Rewards should be commensurate with performance—both individually and nationally. At the individual level, wages (and other forms of income) should temporarily lag behind productivity; at the national level, the exchange rate (dramatically lowered before foreign trade liberalization) must temporarily stay below purchasing power parity. Those two principles are the basis of my recently formulated "hypothesis of two transformation cushions." Weak markets and new private owners need such cushions for some time; the higher the speed of transformation, the thinner the cushions needed (see chapter 11). Indirect methods (restrictive macroeconomic policies) and resistance to excessive demands of trade unions are more important than direct measures (wage regulation).

To summarize, privatization is what distinguishes the first and second stages; it must be accompanied by continuing macroeconomic stabilization and by the rationalization of social policy.

Stage 3

If the "fixing up" suggested in the previous section is successful, something that may be called the early post-transformation stage is reached. The extraordinary, temporary, constructive role of the state is over; it should start to play—once again—a standard, more or less passive, nonconstructivist role.

The country in this early post-transformation stage is, of course, characterized by weak economic and political structures and markets. Their deepening and widening—which cannot be directly done by the state—is the main challenge. The government must try only to eliminate all the barriers to political and economic freedom before the entrepreneurs finally take over and the standard evolutionary process begins.

My country has reached the early post-transformation stage. Of course, the dangers and pitfalls of this stage need our close attention as much as those of the first two stages did.

5. The Role of Vision in the Transformation from Communism to Democratic Capitalism

I am extremely honored to be awarded the James Madison Institute's 1995 International Prize. This is not the first prize or award I have received in the last couple of years, but it is a very special one. For someone who has spent 95 percent of his life in a totalitarian system to get a prize for his achievements in advancing democratic capitalism, and to get it in America, the cradle of liberty, feels like science fiction or a dream, and I have to pinch myself to believe it is true.

I would like to share with you some of my ideas about and experiences with the transition from communism to democratic capitalism; to discuss the roles that the two previous recipients of the prize, Milton Friedman and Michael Novak, have played in our efforts to dismantle socialism (or communism); and, finally, to mention another man whose name is connected with your institute and the prize, James Madison, because of the relevance of his ideas on liberty and federalism to the ongoing process of European integration.

We started to dismantle communism six years ago without the slightest flirtation with the possibility of reforming it. We knew there was no fundamental structural difference between communism and socialism, that the system was not reformable, that there was nothing like socialism with a human face, and that there was no third way between capitalism and socialism. At least in our country, our position on that was clear and straightforward. Soon after the break, my almost innocent remark at the World Economic Forum in Davos that "the third way is the fastest way to the third world" became quite popular.

Speech given at the James Madison Institute Center for World Capitalism, Jacksonville, Florida, December 1, 1995.

We also knew that just saying no to communism would give satisfaction and meaning to life for only a short period of time. We knew that the negative vision of communism had to be very rapidly supplemented with a positive one. In the first issue of your *Review*, published in January 1993, F. R. Livingston recalled an ancient proverb: "Where there is no vision, the people perish." I agree but with some qualification. In the long run they perish, but in the short run they suffer because they are not able to create a functioning and decent system of human society. A positive vision is necessary, even though I am not an advocate of social constructivism (see chapter 4). On the contrary, I am a true believer in the Hayekian idea of evolutionary formation of all complex human institutions, but I know that after the institutions of one social system are dismantled, the institutional vacuum must be rapidly filled with new rules of the game, both formal (laws) and informal (patterns of conduct); otherwise chaos and anarchy start to govern society. Therefore, it was necessary to introduce some elementary, system-creating measures; and the role of vision, suggesting where to go and how to get there, was enormous.

For me, the positive vision coincided with the ideas your institute has been preaching since its establishment. It was a vision of society based on constitutional democracy and political pluralism, on private enterprise and a market economy, and on individual liberty, because that is the only way to protect individuals from the persistent attempts of fanatics, utopians, and demagogues of all colors and "isms" to enforce upon society their own views of human happiness.

I call that capitalism, and I know you call it democratic capitalism. It is probably the same thing, but I am expected to warn against using unnecessary adjectives. Immediately after the collapse of communism, some of my perestroika-favoring countrymen, influenced by the currently fashionable European ideology of "soft" socialism and a patronizing welfare state and supported by similarly oriented American leftists, were fighting for a socialist market economy (that is, against capitalism). My reaction to that was another often-quoted phrase: "market economy without any adjectives." I said that because I know that adjectives make a simple and straightforward concept fuzzy. And recently I was pleased to discover in Irving Kristol's book *Neoconservatism* that he is for "conservatism without adjectival modification."

Anyway, I believe capitalism, of course democratic, is the only system that makes possible material prosperity and political, economic, and human freedom.[1] Capitalism encompasses the economic, political, and moral and cultural (or to put it differently, spiritual) worlds. It is sometimes suggested that those three worlds together, not just one or two of them, constitute democratic capitalism. I would not call those worlds "systems" because I don't believe in the divisibility of human life into compartments. I prefer, therefore, to speak about three dimensions of one system. The logic of human behavior in all of them is identical, and it would be a disaster to accept the accusations of enemies of democratic capitalism who say that economic behavior is egoistic whereas political behavior is or should be altruistic, that economic transactions and morality are incompatible, that culture is noble and superior whereas financial markets are nasty and inferior, and so on. We human beings are consistent and coherent in our behavior, which is exactly what mainstream economics, perhaps in a less explicit way, and the public-choice school, in an explicit and deeper way, keep telling us.

This argument has, at least for me, a general validity, and my recent experience with a profound systemic change at home reinforces it further. We understood very clearly that it was possible neither to change the political system first and the economic system second; nor to decentralize economic decisionmaking but postpone political decentralization; nor to wait for people to be prepared to behave as Schumpeterian innovators before dismantling central planning; nor to educate people first and to liberalize, deregulate, and privatize afterwards (that is exactly what the Russian academicians have been preaching to huge crowds in their highly paid lectures at the American liberal universities since the beginning of perestroika). It is the chicken-egg problem, and it is quite clear that we have to go ahead—simultaneously—in all three dimensions of our lives.

It seems to me that it is appropriate to mention the two people you selected as recipients of the International Prize in the last two years. They had a great influence on our ideas.

---

[1] For a differentiation of the three "freedoms," see Milton Friedman, "Inaugural Lecture: Economic Freedom, Human Freedom, and Political Freedom," Smith Center for Private Enterprise Studies, California State University, Hayward, November 1, 1992.

Milton Friedman—in *Capitalism and Freedom*, in *Free to Choose*, written with Rose Friedman, and in hundreds of both scholarly and popular books and articles—has probably done more than anyone else in this country, or elsewhere, in the last 50 years to straightforwardly expose, explain, and defend the virtues of capitalism.

I am proud to know Friedman personally now (after having read his work for three decades); I am proud of having been called and, of course, accused of being, a monetarist, a Friedmanite, and a Chicagoan even in the dark days of communism, many years before I stepped upon Chicago soil for the first time in 1989. I am proud of having learned the basic tenets of my own thinking from reading his works. I was influenced by his works on methodology (positive vs. normative approach, instrumentalism of scientific assumptions); by his works on money, monetary theory and policy, and inflation; by his refusal of Keynesianism, macroeconomic interventionism, and fine-tuning; by his stress on free trade and a flexible exchange rate regime; by his consistent and powerful advocacy of liberalization, deregulation, and privatization even in the fields that fully belonged for a long time in the domain of public policy; by his strong belief in markets and disbelief in the state and in government bureaucracy.

He helped explain to us that markets—whether they are liked or disliked—emerge wherever and whenever there are gains to be had from exchange. I remember his short essay "Market or Plan?" which was very instrumental in my efforts to understand the functioning of the communist economy.[2] Unsatisfied with the prevailing orthodoxy of the theory of command economies (both the Western, sovietology-style variant and the fully apologetic Soviet-style variant), I noticed that horizontal relations among economic agents in command economies (characterized by various constraints and restrictions, by extremely weak markets, and by loosely defined property rights) played a more important role than vertical relations between planners and the objects of planning (the firms). Friedman realized that (I quote from memory) "the communist economy functions as it does not because of the suppression of markets but because of their existence." Friedman was right—the communist economy produced goods and services, not because of the planners, but in spite of them.

[2]Milton Friedman, "Market or Plan?" Centre for Research into Communist Economies, London, 1984.

And his message was clear: the more unconstrained markets are, the better.

Michael Novak's contribution was different. He tried to fill the, perhaps only supposed, vacuum behind the political and economic aspects of capitalism, the vacuum into which socialists of all colors tried to rush and from where they tried to criticize us. He provided the moral justification of capitalism. He stressed the social side of capitalism by arguing that capitalism helps the poor to escape from poverty better than any other system, especially better than socialism; he stressed that markets themselves are neither moral nor immoral and that self-interest is not a nasty term but a neutral one; he stressed that capitalism is a system supportive of human creativity, a system that gives a chance to the human mind, to wit, invention, discovery, and enterprise, a system based on the ethic of hard work and not on envy.[3]

Novak convincingly argued that "capitalism rewards effort, talent, inventiveness, and luck" but does not guarantee "equal outcomes," because equality is not compatible with "an inventive and dynamic society" and because "equality can be achieved only by abandoning liberty for tyranny."[4] He tried to explain that capitalism is for all of us, not just for the strong, young, successful, and lucky ones, as is often claimed. Standard economics, in one of its most important theorems, says exactly that in David Ricardo's law of comparative advantage. That law does not say that you need an absolute advantage, because relative advantage is sufficient. The law was formulated for countries but is valid for individuals as well. We all have a comparative advantage, and it is our duty to seek to discover and use it.

Novak—theologian, philosopher, and author of novels and essays—helped us to spread our message among intellectuals who do not study economic and political texts and who can afford to criticize capitalism because its successful functioning gives them a chance to live above subsistence levels and the affluence to purchase literary products. Addressing influential opinion makers was very important and should continue because socialism with its utopian

---

[3]Michael Novak, "Capitalism for the Poor, Capitalism for Democracy," *World Capitalism Review* 2, no. 4 (Fall 1994): 4–11.

[4]Michael Novak, "What Wealth Gap?" *Wall Street Journal*, July 11, 1994.

"lightness" remains a constant temptation to those who envy and to those who, as Novak says, "prefer perfect nonexistent things to imperfect real ones."

The prize I am getting tonight is connected with the name of James Madison, the "godfather" of today's U.S. Constitution. As is well known, his contributions to *The Federalist Papers* were concentrated on the institutionalization of checks and balances and on the limitation of legislative power. That is something we—in a similarly revolutionary era of writing constitutions—try to follow. Madison was fighting the tyranny of kings, and we were fighting the tyranny of a totalitarian regime. I can assure you that his famous words, "the ultimate authority resides in the people alone" (*Federalist* no. 46), have become an integral part of our thinking.

Madison sought to fight rampant corruption, mismanagement, and gross incompetence in individual state governments and their interference with national trade. He, therefore, believed in federalism at the expense of the sovereignty of the constituent states. That is extremely relevant to us in Europe today, where there is a tendency toward federalism and increasing centralization. That is a tendency we view with some fear and concern. Madison was very optimistic in that respect; he believed that "federal government will be smaller than the sum of state governments" (*Federalist* no. 45) and that federal government is less susceptible to special interests (paraphrased from *Federalist* no. 10). I don't intend to discuss the U.S. experience, but I am afraid that the experience of the European Union tells us something else. We see more governments and more bureaucrats, we see a more inward-looking (than outward-looking) mentality, we see more room for special interests and rent seeking, we see fewer democratic constraints, and—to come back to the main topic of my discourse—we see more opponents of capitalism in important positions in international institutions than we do at home.

Friedrich von Hayek in his famous essay, "The Intellectuals and Socialism," called our attention to the fact that "in no other field has the predominant influence of the socialist intellectuals together with bureaucrats succeeded in being felt more strongly during the last hundred years than in the contacts between different nations," because intellectuals dominate international relations.[5] That argument is no less true now than it was 46 years ago when it was

---

[5]Friedrich Hayek, "The Intellectuals and Socialism" (1949), in *Studies in Philosophy, Politics, and Economics* (New York: Simon & Schuster, 1969), p. 183.

originally written. If we want a free Europe and if we consider institutions instruments and not goals in themselves, we have to carefully study the consequences of unionistic ideas because "ideas matter."

The idea of democratic capitalism is powerful and sufficiently robust, but it must be continuously exposed, explained, and defended. I agree with Michael Novak that "looking ahead to the twenty-first century, the problem that worries me most is the fragility of free societies."[6] However, the fact that communism collapsed is definitely a good reason for optimism.

[6]Michael Novak, *Awakening from Nihilism*, ed. B. Anderson and D. Cross (Indianapolis: Crisis Books, 1995), p. 41.

6. The Czech Republic: Between the Past and the Future

The Czech Republic, together with other postcommunist countries, has a unique opportunity to create a free society and a free-market economy based on the rejection of both the collectivist and the corporativist or syndicalist approaches to the organization of human society. Let me use this forum to discuss some of the interesting issues of spontaneity and constructivism that lie at the origin of a social order. Only occasionally in the history of a country do circumstances make it possible to start redefining and restructuring the fundamental rules and institutions under which political, economic, and social decisions are made.

That is exactly what we are experiencing, and some of us are deeply involved. In the last five years the key institutions of our society have been in a continuous process of evolutionary emergence and constructive design (and its practical implementation). We have achieved a lot already. The Czech society and economy have progressed to what I call the early post-transformation stage, which can be defined as the stage at which the key transformation tasks have been accomplished.

The old system was totally discredited, its institutions dismantled; and, even more important, the resulting institutional vacuum has been very rapidly filled with an alternative coordinating mechanism. The alternative mechanism is well-known, standard, and noninnovative—political pluralism with free entry into the political market and a market economy based on limited government, private property, liberalization, and deregulation.

It seems almost irrelevant to me now to discuss the transformation stage proper, the intrinsic logic of the changes we have been undergoing, the rules we have had to follow to avoid falling into the

Malcolm Wiener Lecture, Kennedy School of Government, Harvard University, May 2, 1995.

"reform trap" and to minimize the nonnegligible transformation costs. At the beginning, five years ago, I was using an analogy of the game of chess. I begged my fellow countrymen not to ask me what the situation on the chessboard would be after the 25th move of the white bishop. I suggested instead that we test my knowledge of the theoretical opening strategies of the game. The opening is over now. We are well into the middle game. As every chess player knows, the middle game is based less on theory, more on intuition and spontaneity. We are getting closer to the end of the game, but I am sure I still have time to study the well-known ending strategies.

Along the way, we have learned some lessons that may be of interest to students of government and public policy.

We cannot isolate the present from history. For all our preoccupation with the difficult transformation tasks and challenges, it would be wrong and misleading to interpret our situation as a total discontinuity. We live in a very complicated mixture of continuity and discontinuity, and it would be an unforgivable mistake to move society disproportionally to one side of such a multidimensional equation. We have been criticized from both sides, but the art of transforming a society consists exactly in finding the optimum point.

This brings me to a few words about the past. We should neither demonize nor trivialize nor belittle it. Communism was not an unrepeatable event that fell upon its innocent victims without their guilt, their tacit approval, or their active cooperation.

In some respects, structurally, communism was nothing but a more extreme version of the constructivist, paternalistic, and interventionist state whose milder forms are found in Western democratic countries. Our tragic experience helps us to see that very clearly, and that is the main reason for our criticism of some tendencies we see in today's world.

As to the future, we stand firmly—with both our feet—on the ground; we do not want to invent a new, unknown, untried model of the world. We just want to reintroduce into our country the normal, standard world in which you have been privileged to live. I have to stress this point because I am afraid of the dangerous and slippery "third ways" of constructivist attempts to create a Brave New World (to use Aldous Huxley's apt phrase) based on immodest intellectual aspirations. We were victims of such attempts, and we do not want to lose our freedom again.

By "reintroduce," I do not mean return. We are not going back; we know that we cannot turn back the clock of history. We are moving forward, but in a way enriched or constrained by experience and by proven conservative values and traditions.

When I stress normal, standard, and, therefore, generally applicable solutions to political, social, and economic problems of the postcommunist countries, and not only them, I do not deny or underestimate all the diversity of culture, historical heritage, recent experience, natural endowment, climate, and so on; but our tasks and our challenges have undoubtedly more general than specific features.

We believe in the universality of human nature and, along with Adam Smith, in the strong internal motives people have to improve their lives, fates, and well-being. I do not think it is necessary to teach and educate them to modify their dreams, tastes, habits, and preferences because they are their own and not ours. People all over the world are able to use existing opportunities for themselves, and by doing that they magnify opportunities for the rest of us. What we have to do is remove all the barriers, restrictions, and constraints that have been artificially created in the past and establish new rules, new playgrounds, a new environment. We do not intend to perfect men and women; we just want to perfect the institutional framework for their activities. Free society and market economy are universal concepts, and I can assure you that we accept them no less than you do.

When trying to contribute to the creation of a free society, we are confronted with endless criticism, from both within and without, that we have not solved all our inherited problems yet and that our success in dismantling communism is below expectations. I have to argue that those who endorse such a view were either wrong 10 years ago when they considered communism the embodiment of evil, the most undemocratic and inefficient system, or they are wrong now when they suggest that it should have been possible to overcome its legacy at lower costs and much faster. Communism would not have been so evil, so harmful, so extremely inefficient and irrational, had it been possible to get rid of it so easily.

Social phenomena take time. You can—by making unnecessary mistakes—make the transformation period longer, but the whole system cannot be changed overnight. And what must be emphasized is that this is not an intellectual exercise, an attempt to optimize the sequencing of individual transformation measures; it is a multidimensional societal issue in which the spontaneity of human behavior and the complexity of human interaction play crucial roles. Intellectual and, therefore, constructivist reform blueprints are of minor importance.

When we talk—both in our country and elsewhere—about the future, we start with the assumption that the conflict between communism and a free society is over. That may be true, but it does not imply that we have gotten to the end of history or the end of ideology, as is sometimes suggested. As long as human beings remain human beings, there will be ideological conflict.

Present and future conflicts will be no less important, fierce, and dangerous than the conflicts of the past, and we should not underestimate them. Let me mention some of the fashionable issues in the new conflict of visions: free versus fair trade; new forms of and reasons for government regulation connected with organized special interests versus the free market; social or ecological dumping, or both, versus free competition; and communitarianism versus free society.

Opponents of truly free society criticize modern society and the moral decay connected with it, favor many undisputedly good things, play upon a combination of popular anxieties about the future and nostalgia for a partly imaginary past, bring new dreams to our attention, and promise positive outcomes.

I am afraid such approaches—taken together—constitute a real danger to civil liberty because they are directly anti-liberal (in the European meaning of the word). We are in many respects oversensitive to that danger after 40 years of communism. We are aware of the fatal gap (or almost ravine) between good intentions and the methods of imposing them directly upon us. Good ideas should be preached, but preaching yields results in decades or centuries. Advocates of constructivist approaches, however, want a quicker fixing of the world and do not want just to patiently promote their ideas in a standard political process, look for difficult tradeoffs, and try to balance diverging views. The new messengers of truth are too impatient to wait for standard solutions. And we have to caution against that.

The past is definitely over, and we want to avoid falling into the same or similar traps in the future. I have tried to outline the way of thinking that helped us to overcome the past in my country and that is used in the endless struggle for a better future. I am sure you and we will be on the same side of the barricade.

7. Transforming toward a Free Society

This is the fourth consecutive general meeting of our society in which I have participated, and we are still talking about "Transforming toward a Free Society." I hope we will continue talking about it because such a goal can never be fully achieved and, especially, cannot be achieved forever. We all know that it is a permanent task for all of us to fight for a free society regardless of whether we live in a country that is more or less free now or is not, or in a country that experienced a nonfree period in the past or did not. I am convinced that the marginal productivity of our efforts will be positive wherever we live. I am sure we all know that.

It seems to me that, paradoxically, our task in former communist countries may be somewhat easier or, to put it differently, that our task may be more rewarding. The reason is that the marginal improvement in our case is bigger.

I wish to start my remarks today by reminding you of my address to our general meeting in Cannes (see chapter 4). After having reread it recently, I am afraid that I have nothing important or revolutionary to add to it. That may demonstrate either my lack of inspiration or my feeling that at least for practical purposes everything worth saying has already been said.

Two years ago I tried to call your attention to the fact that the transformation—or in another terminology the systemic change— is an *evolutionary process* that is made up of a very complicated mixture of planned and unplanned movements, of intended and unintended events, a process that is based on a rather delicate mixture of intentions and spontaneity—to use Hayek's famous terms. That interpretation of events—however simple and trivial—proved to be very useful for both theoretical discussions and practical policy-making. It was an approach disliked only by those who had immodest ambitions of social engineering and who—after the collapse of

---

Speech given at the 1996 general meeting of the Mont Pèlerin Society, Vienna, September 12, 1996.

communism—tried to make use of a unique opportunity to construct such a complex phenomenon as a new social system and to fine-tune its emergence. The members of the Mont Pèlerin Society have been—for five decades already—warning against all kinds of left-wing social constructivism (that has been, after all, one of our strongest messages), but I am afraid that, even a few years ago, some of us tended to make a similar mistake. We should have known that capitalism—defined as a market economy based on private property and minimal government and a constitutional democracy based on the rule of law and the unconstrained competition of political parties—cannot be "introduced." We should have known that it must evolve, grow, gain strength, and mature in the way described by some of our distinguished members, notably Hayek, not to speak of our great-grandfathers like Adam Smith.

When discussing transformation from communism (not from an interventionist welfare state), I suggest starting with the nontrivial idea that the communist system collapsed, that it was not defeated. It collapsed because it was in an advanced stage of decomposition, because it gradually lost its two strongest constitutive elements—*fear* and *faith*. In its final days, the communist system became both soft and unconvincing, and such a state of affairs was not sufficient for safeguarding its further continuation. It is an irony of history that communism sort of "melted down," something of which some of our brave colleagues in the postcommunist world do not like to be reminded. Part of their aura would be lost, and that is the reason why they try to contest such an interpretation of events. But I am convinced that it is correct.

We are being confronted with the idea that the collapse of communism created a vacuum. At first glance that seems plausible, but it is not. What remained was not a vacuum. We inherited weak and, therefore, inefficient markets and a weak and inefficient democracy. Both the economic and the political mechanisms were shallow. The political and economic agents (players of the game) were not properly defined and established; they were new, weak, and fragile, and the outcomes of their interplay were, therefore, less efficient than in a full-grown free society as you know it in countries that have never experienced communism and where the spontaneous, evolutionary (Hayekian) process of institution building and agent formation has never been interrupted. In spite of that, there was no need (not to mention no possibility) to fill a vacuum with a ready-made, imported-from-outside system. We had to move at the margin and make incremental changes. No masterminding of the evolution of a free society was possible.

On the other hand, I agree with those who make the point that it was not possible to wait for a sufficient degree of market efficiency. The quick abolition of old institutions was a sine qua non for success because it was the only way to minimize the nonnegligible transition costs. At the beginning the weak markets were not more efficient than the command economy that existed before, but that should not become an argument against early liberalization and deregulation measures. Consistency in pursuing a free-market course was crucial, and the government had to help by introducing some pro-market, pro-competition measures, but strictly in the Euckenian, *Ordo*-liberal way.[1] The absence of such positive policy would have been costly and therefore counterproductive. We had to privatize (instead of passively waiting for the emergence of new private ventures), to liberalize, and to deregulate as fast as possible.

The relative weakness or strength of institutions of a newly formed free society is only one aspect of the whole issue. What about the people? Are they ready for such rapid change? Does free society presuppose—in addition to the creation of its basic institutions—some set of values or moral standards that would properly anchor the society? Do the people need an interim period of "schooling"? Is such schooling realizable? Are there suitable teachers? Are the people ready to be educated? My answer to those and similar questions is simple. The people are always ready, and they do not need a special education. What they need is a free space for their voluntary activities, the elimination of controls and prohibitions of all kinds.

The title of this morning's session is "Transforming toward a Free Society." What kind of free society do we have in mind? Should we transform ourselves toward a theoretical model of free society or toward a real free society as we see it in many forms in Western Europe and North America? Theoretically, the answer is very simple and straightforward. The closer we get to the ideal case, the better. In reality, it is more complicated. Whenever I try at home to avoid

---

[1]The journal *Ordo*, the primary organ of mainstream German postwar liberalism, was founded in 1948 by Walter Eucken and Franz Böhm.

introducing illiberal legislation or to repeal an existing illiberal law, I am reminded of the same law in one Western country after another, or—recently more and more often—I am told that what I do not want to accept is the recent recommendation or instruction of the European Commission. Our "submissiveness" in this respect (and now I do not pretend to deny that my country is still in a rudimentary stage of its evolution as compared to some "old" democracies) can become, paradoxically, a constraint on our spontaneous evolution toward a free society.

After the collapse of "hard" communism, we rejected reformed communism, we avoided romantic nationalism (with its very negative systemic consequences), we overcame utopian attempts to forget everything and to start building a Brave New World based on a priori moralistic and elitist ambitions (of those who are better than the rest of us). Our remaining task is to not succumb to the kind of statist, interventionist, paternalistic social democracy that we see in so many free societies to the west of us.

We know that it is our task to attack the expanding state, which was, and still is, a dominant tendency of the 20th century, of the century of socialisms with a variety of confusing adjectives. The majority of intellectuals and social scientists of this century considered that tendency almost an iron law of history. We have to demonstrate that it is possible to make a return to the liberal social order.

The farther east one travels, the more problematic may be the prospects for a rapid transition. But traveling west is not without problems, either. The best direction is toward the Mont Pèlerin world, but finding the way is not easy.

PART II

THE CZECH EXPERIENCE

8. The Ten Commandments of Systemic Reform

The Czech Republic has been realizing the most radical, the fastest, and the most consistent and comprehensive economic (and social) transformation in the whole postcommunist world. In addition, the Czech Republic was successful in creating a standard, pluralistic political system, and in last year's parliamentary elections the country supported market-oriented democratic and liberal political leaders. Prospects for the Czech Republic—regardless of the repeated negative impact of external factors—are positive, and the overall situation is stable both economically and socially.

In the last three years we have learned some lessons that may be of interest to other reforming countries. I call them the "Ten Commandments" for profound, fundamental, structural (or systemic) reform.

First Commandment

In such a fundamental change of a whole society there can be no purely economic solution. Social engineers' dreams of organizing or masterminding the whole process of a systemic transformation are wrong, misleading, and dangerous. The theoretical analysis of optimal sequencing of individual reform steps that we may find and study in sophisticated economic journals is of academic interest only, because the reality is and will always be different. Unavoidable time lags, political and social pressures exerted by various vested interests, human failures, and the unimaginable complexities of the whole transformation process make it impossible to centrally plan the origin and rise of a market economy.

Luncheon address delivered to the plenary meeting of the Group of Thirty, Vienna, April 1993.

Second Commandment

The role of foreign aid in the transformation process is marginal at most; the reform must be undertaken at home, and we have had time and opportunity to understand that to ask for foreign aid in the increasingly egoistic and protectionist world of the last decade of the 20th century is a useless activity. My everyday experience in the last three years with the ambiguities of foreign assistance confirms the standard textbook criticisms of development aid.

Third Commandment

There is absolutely no way to avoid the transformational shakeout of nonviable economic activities sustained by subsidized prices, artificial demand, and sheltered markets. No macroeconomic management (fiscal or monetary fine-tuning, or both) can eliminate a decline in gross domestic product, an increase in unemployment, a one-time price jump (after price deregulation), and a drastic devaluation (before liberalization) of foreign trade. Rational macroeconomic policy can, however, avoid permanent galloping inflation, repeated devaluations, state budget deficits, and growing foreign indebtedness.

Fourth Commandment

Detailed plans for organized sequencing of reform measures have no chance of success in the real world, but several basic macrorules should be followed. If we—for the sake of simplicity—disregard political and social factors, our experience tells us that we have to start with a heavy dose of restrictive macroeconomic policy, which prepares the ground for price and foreign trade liberalization and— by cutting subsidies—announces a dramatic change in the whole economic climate. A reforming country that does not realize this crucial measure early inevitably falls into what I call the reform trap: a vicious circle of high inflation (or even hyperinflation), repeated devaluations, growing foreign indebtedness, budget deficits, and the like. (I believe that the country that deliberately—without International Monetary Fund pressure—and most vigorously implemented this unpopular step was, undoubtedly, Czechoslovakia.)

The next step is a merciless price and foreign trade liberalization that unlocks markets, returns proper "values" to economic assets— to all goods and services—changes past demand patterns, creates economic equilibrium and market clearing, and gives necessary signals to the (still mostly unreconstructed) economic agents operating on the supply side of the economy. The exchange rate must become a solid nominal anchor, the only stable, unchanging nominal variable. Because of huge structural defects of the economy (reflected in balance-of-payments deficits), the exchange rate must be, however, very far from purchasing power parity. Price liberalization must be complete (or at least very far advanced); otherwise new price distortions are created. Wage regulation should be based on indicative guidelines or nonexistent. Foreign trade liberalization must be accompanied by internal convertibility of the devalued currency.

Having withstood requests for help, for bailing out, for markets, for subsidies, for modernization and restructuring of state-owned firms, the government must initiate a rapid and comprehensive privatization process as a precondition for further changes, as a mechanism for finding real (and, therefore, responsible and rationally behaving) owners, as a final blow to the ambitions of government bureaucrats to control the economy.

Other reform measures (tax reform, new legislation, improvement of market structures, the rise of financial intermediaries and other market-type institutions) can be undertaken any time they are prepared and ready for implementation.

Those basic sequencing rules are neither original nor innovative; such ideas may seem original only because they are so often forgotten or ignored.

Fifth Commandment

The delicate task (complicated by the existence of a fully independent central bank and by rapid changes in both the velocity of money and the demand for money) is to find the right moment for the shift in macroeconomic policy—from a restrictive one to a neutral or, perhaps, even an expansionary one. The economy, undergoing such a radical transformation, is far from homogeneous; the turning point on the aggregate supply curve—from the horizontal to the vertical segment of the curve—is, therefore, very sharp and is located far below the full-employment level. Populist pressures to inflate the economy are very strong, but they must be resisted. We spent the first two years—before and immediately after price liberalization—in a restrictive policy (budget surplus) regime; then we moved to a neutral, balanced-budget policy regime; and we continue to follow that course. It seems to me that no transforming economy has reached the stage where it would be appropriate to release fiscal and monetary controls and to begin to implement Keynesian-like, demand-expanding policies.

Sixth Commandment

The inevitable price shock that follows price deregulation must be announced and explained ahead of time, defended, and "survived." The original price increase reflects the magnitude of the inherited macroeconomic disequilibrium (small in Czechoslovakia but huge in Poland, Russia, and other ex–Soviet Union countries), whereas the postderegulation price dynamics reflect the degree of restrictiveness of the current fiscal-monetary mix. In the case of Czechoslovakia, the initial (first month) price increase (inflation) was "only" 25 percent; in the following three months the rate of inflation dropped to 7 percent, 4.5 percent, and then 2 percent, and in the following 20 months (till the introduction of the value-added tax at the beginning of 1993) the rate of inflation never exceeded 1 percent per month. In other reforming countries inflation has fluctuated and fluctuates heavily; there were repeated inflation peaks and troughs— reflecting inconsistencies in macroeconomic policy.

Two debilitating vicious circles must be avoided if reform is to continue: price-wage and price–exchange rate spirals. Our experience tells us that the appearance of both is closely connected with the unnecessary failure of macroeconomic policy. In the period of the restrictive policy regime (1990–91) wages in our country were growing slower than prices; under the "neutral" macroregime (1992–93) wages have been growing slightly faster, but the dangerous range has not yet been reached, and the wage variable has been moving consistently with other linked economic variables.

The same holds for the price–exchange rate nexus. Reforming countries usually simultaneously face a high degree of macrodisequilibrium (huge price increases, therefore, are unavoidable), overvalued currency (with zero hard currency reserves and large balance-of-payment deficits), and budget deficits (because of loose macroeconomic policies). Nevertheless, the typical reforming country does not devalue its currency sufficiently; growing domestic prices tend to discourage exports and encourage imports; the balance of payments deteriorates; new devaluation is necessary; imported inflation (because of devaluation) pushes prices upward; and the dangerous vicious circle is unavoidable. In Czechoslovakia the situation was and is different. The original macrodisequilibrium was relatively small, macropolicy was cautiously restrictive, and devaluation was sufficiently deep. The high rate of devaluation created enough room for necessary price (and other cost) increases, and the exchange rate has, therefore, already been stable for 28 months in spite of 75 percent price inflation that occurred in the same period. In addition, hard currency reserves have been growing. That demonstrates that the vicious circle can be avoided—provided rational economic policy is followed.

Seventh Commandment

The economy cannot be restructured without a comprehensive shift in the property rights structure. To expect a change in economic agents' behavior without privatization is unwarranted; it never happens. The perestroika style of economic thinking—reaching its most sophisticated form in Hungarian János Kornai's pamphlets—has wrong and misleading policy implications. The shift from a soft budget constraint to a hard one cannot be achieved by macroeconomic measures only. Rational macroeconomic policy represents a necessary, but not a sufficient, condition for desired changes in economic behavior.

The reforming country needs to organize a rapid and massive privatization that can be achieved only when the government follows several nontraditional rules:

- Standard, therefore slow, privatization methods must be accompanied by much faster nonstandard ones.
- The aim of privatization is to find new, private owners, not to maximize the government's revenue from the sale of government assets.
- Privatization must start at the microlevel, not at the government level. A special government agency should perform procedural functions only; no planning, organizing, modernizing, restructuring, dividing, or demonopolizing functions should be initiated from above (Germany is an extreme example of such an approach).

- Foreign capital involvement is appreciated, but foreign capital should not be preferentially treated vis-à-vis domestic capital. The role of foreign advisers and consultants should be minimized.

The Czechoslovak voucher privatization method was extremely successful and should be tried in other countries. It is difficult to block activities of government privatization agencies, especially their attempts to bureaucratically control (and distort) the whole privatization process.

Eighth Commandment

The basic reform strategy should be based on a maximum degree of sharing of nontrivial transformation costs. The concept of sharing is necessary for social reasons (to make it possible to advocate the inevitably growing disparities in income and property) as well as for economic reasons (to bear jointly the inherited burden of excessive inventories of unsalable products; of old, bad loans; of unfinished investment projects; of unreturnable, frozen assets in foreign countries; and the like). The problem is the tendency to shift the transformation costs to the government, which becomes the payor of last resort. Its degree of freedom to make positive, "autonomous" decisions (and financial outlays) becomes smaller and smaller, and its involuntary, induced expenditures dominate the state budget.

Ninth Commandment

I have already mentioned the crucial role of domestic factors in the transformation process and the limited impact of foreign aid and advice. The external dimension is, however, extremely significant in another respect. What we really need from the rest of the world is not aid; it is trade and exchange. By exchange I mean symmetrical relations based on the principle of equivalence. We do not need one-way transfers because they are usually not taken seriously by either side. They tend to be misused, misdirected, or misplaced. We do need, however, exchange of people, of ideas, and most important, of goods, organized in such a way that both sides of the deal benefit. That is why we are so critical of the discriminatory and protectionist measures that are taken in response to any success of our exports in Western markets. Paradoxically, the transformation of the post-communist countries in Europe represents a very important external challenge for Western Europe as well. It becomes evident that the collapse of the iron curtain does not necessitate restructuring and transformation on the eastern side only. The western side needs to adjust as well, and the necessity of doing so is no less urgent. Attempts to postpone this painful economic and social process by protectionism and by trade discrimination against former communist countries can only worsen problems on both sides.

Tenth Commandment

It is absolutely necessary for the reformers to believe in the reforms if they are to succeed in inspiring their fellow citizens and be able to create broad pro-reform coalitions. Reform is not an academic problem; it is a political issue, and it is vitally important to win for it sufficient political support. We understood at the very beginning that building a political base was an indispensable component of reform. We succeeded in creating the only classical-liberal party in the former communist world that is able to address the people and get wide political support. It required enormous activity, hundreds of political rallies, and endless meetings with thousands of people— in another words, it required and still requires permanent campaigning. Telling the truth was a major weapon that helped us to win elections and create a basic reform-supporting consensus. A credible program, not populism; realism, not false promises; optimism and self-confidence instead of pessimism, doomsday scenarios, and dreams of state paternalism are preconditions for success. We hope we will have it.

9. The Ten Commandments of Systemic Reform Revisited

The Czech Republic, together with other Central and Eastern European countries, has a unique opportunity now to create a free society and a free-market economy. We are, all of us, aware of that. And we know we cannot afford to miss the chance to do it, because such an opportunity comes once in a century.

The communist system was totally discredited in most of the former communist countries; its institutions have been dismantled and, even more important, the resulting institutional vacuum has been filled—with different results in individual countries—with an alternative coordinating mechanism. In my country the mechanism we have introduced is political pluralism with free entry into the political market and a market economy based on a limited government, private property, liberalization, and deregulation.

We spent almost half a century in a communist society, and to get rid of it, we initiated a radical transformation process during which the key institutions of our society have been changing continuously. As you know, we have already achieved a lot. Czech society has progressed to what I call the early post-transformation stage, which can be defined as the point at which the key transformation tasks have been accomplished.

After almost six years of radical restructuring of the whole economic system (with a very interesting interplay of political and social factors), we can begin to draw some lessons or at least make some preliminary generalizations about the whole process. More than two years ago, at the meeting of the Group of Thirty in Vienna, I presented my tentative "Ten Commandments of Systemic Reform"

The 1995 International Finance Corporation Annual Lecture, Washington, D.C., December 4, 1995. Earlier versions of this lecture were delivered at the plenary meeting of the Group of Thirty in Vienna, April 1993 (chapter 8), to the European Economic Association congress in Prague, September 1995, and as the SBC Warburg Annual Lecture in London, September 18, 1995.

(chapter 8). Tonight I would like to present, not a revision of my original ideas, but a more or less new, up-to-date version of them.

First Commandment

At the beginning, immediately after the collapse of the communist political, social, and economic system, we were confronted with what I would now call, with some overstatement, the impossibility theorem. We were told that everybody knew how to transform capitalism into socialism (or how to turn fish into fish soup) but that nobody knew how to transform socialism into democracy, political pluralism, individual responsibility, private property, and a market economy. We were warned on all sides that the books on how to do so had not yet been written, that the relevant theory was not available, that we would have to wait for the formulation of a new economics of transformation, that the people were not prepared for such a radical change, that they had to be educated in advance, and so on and so forth.

Nonsense. The people are always prepared; the sleeping *Homo oeconomicus* is immediately ready to grasp new opportunities. And the politicians are not lost, either. All the knowledge of what to do is here. It is described in elementary textbooks, and it is hidden in many similar experiences in the past. The transformation process is, however, not an exercise in applied economics. It has its own logic and dynamics, and the task of reformers is to make it possible. Systemic change is a very fragile mixture of spontaneity and intentions, of the utility-maximizing behavior of millions of free human beings and system-transforming measures initiated and organized by political authorities (see chapter 4). It is sufficient to avoid measures that go against it.

Second Commandment

We were told that there was something like optimal sequencing of reform measures. Such advice was and is not correct. I do not deny the existence of some elementary rules that should be, if possible, followed. But to claim that there is something other than that, that there is something like the scientific masterminding of transformation measures, is wrong.

The relevant recommendations in this regard can be summarized as follows:

- Whenever there is an opportunity to introduce a new measure, it should be done without the slightest delay, because a better time never comes.
- Before completely eliminating the old coordinating mechanism, the old rules of the game, the macroeconomic situation (both fiscal and monetary policies) must be under firm control; otherwise only chaos and anarchy will follow.
- Liberalization and deregulation measures should be radical, fast, and predominant; otherwise new economic distortions and imbalances will be introduced.
- Privatization, which represents the final dividing line between the old and the new systems, must be done with the help of nonstandard, and therefore much faster, methods than the International Finance Corporation would like; where the process is slower, preprivatization agony threatens to become the main obstacle to successful restructuring of individual firms as well as of the whole economy.

Third Commandment

The economics profession was, for a long time, led astray by a false dilemma—gradualism versus shock therapy—that was based on several wrong assumptions. It was assumed that speed itself means shock therapy, which is not true. It was also assumed that rapid change is more painful and more costly and gradualism less painful and less costly. It is, however, clear to all of us now that the slower the process of transformation, the more costly and the more painful it is and the less chance it has for success.

It was further assumed that there is a choice between shock therapy and gradualism. That is not true because various transformation measures have different time requirements (e.g., price and foreign trade liberalization can be done overnight, but privatization takes years to complete). Things have to be done whenever they can be done, or at least they have to be prepared without any delay. The real choice is between transformation and nontransformation, between success and failure.

Fourth Commandment

The elimination or termination of economic activities that do not meet a demand in the new economic system and in the changed international setting is inevitable. The resulting decline in gross domestic product should not be interpreted as an economic crisis or a recession, which could have been avoided by better macromanagement. Such a decline is part of a healthy process of forming a viable economic structure and of creating an economic equilibrium. It would have been easier to minimize loss of output if only one country had been undergoing such a transformation process; but the deep economic decline that followed the total collapse of COMECON (the Council for Mutual Economic Assistance) should not be considered a symptom of failure. The faster and deeper the decline, the better. Nevertheless, opposite assertions are frequently found in popular as well as economic literature and in statements of prominent international institutions.

Fifth Commandment

Liberalizing prices after half a century of price rigidity (and of forced savings and especially of forced substitution) brings about a one-time price increase plus moderate inflation (moderate, if economic fundamentals are in order). Subsequent inflation is the result of continuing deregulation of prices (because price liberalization is not total) on the one hand and of rapid and frequent adjustments at the microlevel on the other hand. Because of that, core inflation has for some time a nonzero value regardless of the macrosituation. The high rate of inflation we see in most of the transforming countries is, however, the result of macromismanagement, of irresponsible fiscal or monetary policies, or both.

Sixth Commandment

We are confronted with a popular but misleading idea that the rate of unemployment is positively correlated with the rate of economic restructuring. Such an economic law does not exist, and in my opinion it can find neither theoretical nor empirical support. The faster the process of systemic transformation, of privatization and restructuring of individual firms, of liberalization and deregulation, the lower the rate of unemployment. In a standard market economy it is rigidity, not flexibility, that produces unemployment, and the same is true for countries undergoing transformation.

Seventh Commandment

The behavior of two variables, wages and the exchange rate, is of crucial importance. There is no way to avoid the real wage decline that accompanies the decline of GDP. It is an advantage that the collapse of old communist institutions has weakened labor organizations, trade unions, chambers of commerce, confederations of industries, and other similar rent-seeking organizations. The fundamental systemic change must be accomplished before they recapture their power and start wage disputes. (This is, by the way, an additional argument for maximum speed in the whole transformation process.)

Because prices move faster than do wages, price and wage liberalization—together with a restrictive fiscal and monetary policy—pushes real wages down (more than can be explained by the actual decline in GDP). That helps to establish internal equilibrium, and, in addition, it creates a breathing space for newly formed (or restructured) firms. That creates a totally new economic situation. The first of two important transformation cushions—as I call them—is created: real wages are temporarily pushed below the productivity of labor.

At the same time, devaluation of the currency—necessary for achieving external equilibrium—pushes the exchange rate below purchasing power parity. That creates the second transformation cushion.

Those two cushions guarantee that

- the economic situation in the country is stable; it is characterized by relatively low inflation, balance-of-payments stability, growing hard currency reserves, and no foreign indebtedness;
- relatively low wages and a relatively favorable exchange rate increase competitiveness and help firms to survive the critical transformation maneuver;
- a fall into a dangerous devaluation trap can be avoided (on the contrary, stability of the nominal exchange rate brings about a permanent real revaluation);
- real wages can constantly go up during the whole transformation process.

Transformation cushions should not last forever. Because of the rapid growth of nominal wages and because of more rapid inflation than in member countries of the Organization for Economic Cooperation and Development, they are getting thinner and thinner and will ultimately disappear.

Eighth Commandment

The post-transformation recovery cannot be made sharper (or start earlier), and when it happens, it brings about new problems:

- It makes the disinflation task more difficult.
- It creates tensions in the labor market.
- It accelerates imports and diverts domestic output from exports, resulting in a balance-of-trade (and subsequently a current account) deficit. Such a deficit cannot be eliminated by government intervention (pro-export and anti-import policies would not do so). It must be temporarily financed. Using a portion of the capital account surplus to do so is quite appropriate.

Ninth Commandment

Privatization is of crucial importance. I have tried for years to stress both at home and abroad the profound difference between what I call "transformation privatization" and "classical privatization" (see chapter 12). The task of transformation privatization is to privatize standard firms and, by doing so, to prepare the economy for classical privatization (à la Margaret Thatcher). Transformation privatization in my country is over, but political as well as academic critics are saying that by privatizing we have not succeeded in forming an optimum property rights structure. The goal of transformation privatization was not to complete the restructuring of property rights but, on the contrary, to be its beginning. The task of government at that moment was to find the first private owners, not the final ones. That fundamental difference tends to be misunderstood (partly because it reflects belief in the potency of government intervention and disbelief in the spontaneity of the market).

Tenth Commandment

Radical political, social, and economic restructuring gives us a unique opportunity not only to dismantle the old communist institutions but also to avoid establishing new barriers to economic freedom. I have in mind, not barriers that were part of the old collectivist ideology, but barriers that can frequently be found in Western countries at the present time.

We are—all of us—confronted with the excesses of welfare state paternalism, with overregulation, with overly ambitious programs to subsidize producers as well as consumers, with corporatist and syndicalist tendencies, with rent seeking and lobbying, with protectionism based both on old arguments and on accusations of social and ecological dumping, and with many other similar phenomena. They are not part of a coherent ideology. They just "happened," and it is difficult to get rid of them. The transforming countries have a historic opportunity not to let them dominate the lives of their citizens.

10. Economic Transformation of the Czech Republic: The Challenges That Remain

In the last couple of years I have made several attempts to discuss—in a more theoretical way—the transformation of a former communist country into a free society with a market economy. My texts were widely published and discussed, both at home and abroad. Moreover, I was lucky to have an opportunity to convert some of the ideas of liberal (I use the term in its original European meaning) economists and other thinkers in the social sciences into practice.

We in the Czech Republic have—after almost seven years of radical restructuring of the whole political, social, and economic system—completed one difficult stage of the transformation process. The relevant questions now are: How to continue? Is the transformation over? Is there—in our situation—a special role for the government as compared to its role in standard countries of the West? What are the new challenges? What remains to be done?

There is no doubt that our society—in all its dimensions—is very different from what it used to be in the communist era. Some changes are visible at first glance, some not. There have probably been more changes in the "software" than in the "hardware" of the whole socioeconomic system, which may confuse some observers, but I am sure that the overall political, economic, and social restructuring went better than had been expected (and not only in the Czech Republic).

In 1993 (and with some modifications again in 1995), I formulated my ten commandments for a systemic reform, and I am quite happy that it is not yet necessary to rewrite them. They included the following postulates:

Speech given at the Institute of International Finance, Washington, D.C., September 29, 1996.

- The fundamental transformation of a whole society in a historically short period is feasible (which is not trivial because six or seven years ago when we started, many doubted that it was possible).
- There is no way to mastermind the whole transformation process and to accomplish optimal sequencing of individual transformation measures.
- There is, in reality, no choice between so-called shock therapy and gradualism. Both terms are gross simplifications suitable for journalists' discussions; they should not be used in a serious debate.
- The crowding out of inviable economic activities (and the consequent economic decline) is an inevitable part of the transformation process.
- An important role is played by very early price liberalization, which must be straightforward and wide ranging. The same is true of foreign trade liberalization.
- There is no economic law saying that the faster the economic restructuring (and privatization), the higher the rate of unemployment (just the opposite is true).
- Two economic variables—wages and the exchange rate—are of crucial importance. At the very beginning of the transformation process they must be pushed down by restrictive macroeconomic policies to create "transformation cushions."
- The post-transformation recovery and long-awaited catching-up process cannot be artificially accelerated or shifted in time.
- The rapid transformation privatization, which is something conceptually different from classical privatization, must be done at a very early stage of the whole process.
- The radical transformation (in a unique and nonrepeatable political atmosphere) should be used not only to dismantle the old institutions of a command economy but also to avoid establishing the institutions of a paternalistic, overregulated welfare state.

That is—in a very condensed form—both a *normative blueprint* and a *positive description* of the transformation process in the Czech Republic. We are now in a situation that can be described as follows:

- The economy has been mostly privatized; the share of state ownership is relatively small and declining; mass privatization is over. We have entered the era of serious ownership restructuring, which will lead to a gradual improvement of corporate governance and of companies' efficiency.

- The government is trying to avoid being involved in any form of microintervention, but the pressures of special interests, of lobbyists of all kinds, of corporativism and syndicalism, of patterns of paternalism imported from abroad are getting stronger because—after their initial weakness—those pressure groups have become consolidated and their strength has grown.

- The economy has started to grow; all macroeconomic figures (expressed in rates of growth) have positive signs, and an economic growth rate of around 5 percent per annum seems to be a feasible middle-term prospect.

- The main bottleneck on the supply side is the low unemployment rate (around 3 percent) and the resulting shortage of labor and net inflow of foreign workers, which slows the rate of economic growth in the short run.

- Relatively strong overall growth, low unemployment, rapid growth of wages, residual deregulation of prices, rapid adjustments of domestic prices to world prices, frequent changes in the structure of the economy with corresponding movements of relative prices, and the like bring about the continuation of an inflation rate of 8 to 10 percent per annum, and further disinflation becomes very difficult.

- More than 60 months of a fixed nominal exchange rate (from the end of 1990 to February 1996) together with a large inflow of foreign capital and a positive balance of payments constrained the monetary policy of the central bank and made it more or less passive (which may be a good way to discipline ambitious monetary authorities). The introduction of a relatively wide margin for fluctuation of the exchange rate in the spring of 1996 changed the situation sharply. It led to a slowdown of the growth of the money supply in the summer and autumn of 1996, which may be a positive contribution to the overall macroeconomic situation.

- Strong demand for money, attempts to slow down the growth of the supply of money, the fragility of the banking sector, plus the financial weakness of many new, privatized, or still state-owned firms keep both real interest rates and margins between interest rates on credits and deposits relatively high, which becomes another inflationary factor (of the cost-push variety).

- Fiscal policy is based on the undisputed goal of a balanced budget and plays, in our context, a highly stabilizing role; the government budget is a continuously decreasing share of gross domestic product.

- Rapid economic growth, very liberal import policies, comparative advantages of foreign firms in entering the Czech market (because of their economic strength they are able to start from better positions), subsidized products from the European Union (with the backing of various methods of export promotion)— all of that pushes domestic demand for imports above the level of exports, which has led to a significant deficit in the balance of trade (which is only partially offset by a positive balance of services). Exports are, moreover, very vulnerable to world (especially European) economic conditions, to various kinds of import restrictions, and to insufficient domestic promotion of exports. The trade deficit is, therefore, considered the most important single economic problem of the current period.

Until now I have been looking at the economy from the purely domestic side. I wish to say a few words about noneconomic issues and about the role of the external side of all of that now.

Until very recently, the relative speed and smoothness of the Czech transformation process (social and political stability, low inflation and unemployment, more or less balanced and "just" sharing of the transformation costs by the whole society, the ingenious voucher privatization method, and so on) guaranteed basic support for the sometimes popular, sometimes painful transformation measures.

Czech society accepted (and "survived") the negative "collapse effect" of the dismantling of old institutions and activities and absorbed—with satisfaction—the positive "liberalization effects" connected with the opening of domestic and foreign markets (not only in the economic sense). Czech society now sees growing disparities in income and property (not everyone is on the winning side) and waits for a massive "wealth effect" of a normally functioning capitalist society and economy. In addition to that, inflation is more stubborn than everyone expected, voucher privatization is over, and more and more groups in society are managing to avoid paying their share of transformation costs. Those who cannot escape paying the costs blame the government for not defending them sufficiently—regardless of the apparent overall economic growth. As a result, basic (more or less unstructured and unconditional) popular support for government policies has begun to vanish, as was reflected in the results of the recent Czech parliamentary elections. The space for brave government measures is, therefore, narrower than before.

Finally, a few words on the role of the rest of the world in this complicated process:

Basic political support, macroeconomic stand-by arrangements, and direct help were extremely important, especially at the beginning. They are of secondary importance now. I do not deny the importance of learning from others, but I have to insist that learning by doing (which means direct involvement in business with foreigners) has been much more important than professional consulting and advisory activity, because the latter is a two-way process and the former is a one-way, nonbinding, unfocused, nonmarket one.

The major external obstacle to our development is the various forms of protectionism we face in foreign markets, in markets of EU countries, in some of the Central European Free-Trade Agreement countries, as well as other developed or developing nations. Despite all the promising rhetoric, the results are not that good. The current fashionable idea of fair trade instead of free trade may become very dangerous.

It is our duty, the duty of all of us, to promote free trade as much as possible on both sides of the foreign trade equation—not only on the import side (which is a usual argument), but on the export side as well (by abolishing all forms of state subsidies and export promotion).

Foreign investors are extremely important, but they should not expect advantages vis-à-vis domestic firms. To give foreign investors advantages is not the way to build a healthy economy.

We wish to be a full member of the European Union (not an external observer). This is serious and, at home, undisputed. Membership in the European Union remains, therefore, our most important external challenge.

11. Radical Economic Reforms in the Czech Republic

Systemic transformation—from a communist totalitarian society to a system of political pluralism and a market economy—is a process based on the complicated interplay of political and economic factors, a process that has a nonzero time dimension and requires a nonaccidental ordering of various transformation measures. The four years after the Velvet Revolution in November 1989 were filled with hard work and also with a lot of positive results.

I would like to share with you a combination of theoretical ideas and practical experience gained in the roles of minister of finance and prime minister. Last year, at the meeting of the prestigious Group of Thirty in Vienna, I formulated the "Ten Commandments of Systemic Transformation" (see chapter 8), which were then published in various languages in many countries. In each of my speeches since then, I have tried to broaden and expound on those commandments. I would like to do that again today. But first, a broader overview of some noneconomic issues (see chapter 2).

Success in the transformation endeavor depends on how well three tasks in three conceptionally different fields are accomplished. The first is a more or less ideological task, the formulation of a clear vision, that is, a vision of a future society in which we wish to live.

The second, which is essentially a political task, is the building of a broad popular consensus in support of the vision. This is not possible without "marketing" the vision through the standard mechanism of political parties' interacting in a parliamentary democracy.

Third, one must understand the peculiarities of the transition period and have the ability to implement the appropriate reform

Address delivered at the Hebrew University, Jerusalem, February 1994. Earlier versions were given at the University of Guadalajara, Mexico, October 1993, and at the Czech Economic Society, Prague, November 1993.

strategy courageously and forcefully, though at the same time carefully, flexibly, and with due respect for those social groups that are the short-term losers during such a process. This is mainly an economic task.

It is necessary to stress that the economic change that takes place in systemic transformation is not perestroika. It is not a change in exogenously given rules that govern the behavior of economic agents at both the micro- and the macrolevel but a fundamental change of ownership rights; it is the decisive elimination of microeconomic decisionmaking by the state; it is relieving markets of their bureaucratic constraints; it is opening ourselves to the world.

Transformation concerns the whole system and therefore is neither modernization nor reconstruction nor the financial stabilization of individual firms; all of those are post-transformation tasks. Systemic transformation is first and mainly about privatization.

That is the reason why privatization has a specific role in the whole transformation process, which makes it different from privatization in the West (see chapter 12). In Western countries privatization is an almost standard "business" aimed at restructuring an individual firm. In our country privatization is part of a systemic transformation. Such privatization has, therefore, a lot of specifics, including the following:

- a mixture of standard and nonstandard privatization methods;
- a different role for the price of privatized firms (and for the state's privatization revenues), and different ways of evaluating privatized firms;
- finding an owner who will perform postprivatization restructuring, instead of a state bureaucrat who tries to restructure the firm before privatization;
- minimization of the length of preprivatization agony, because there is no way to rationalize the behavior of firms waiting for privatization (without reintroducing central planning).

Our country came to understand that better than other countries, and that is the reason why we invented and realized coupon (or voucher) privatization, which is—for many reasons—the catalyst for our whole transformation process.

That process, of course, has—apart from its privatization dimension—its macroeconomic, liberalization, and deregulation dimensions. They also have important, nontrivial rules. Very briefly we
can mention a few, relatively broadly accepted, ideas:

1. Basic macroeconomic stabilization has to be carried out before
   the liberalization of prices and foreign trade (that is, before
   liberalization of internal and external markets).
2. Liberalization of prices and foreign trade must be carried out
   at the same time; otherwise the behavior of inherited monopolies or oligopolies can endanger the whole process.
3. Liberalization of foreign trade must be realized after a significant devaluation of the currency, and it must be accompanied
   by introduction of internal convertibility of the currency.
4. Liberalization and deregulation steps must be as extensive as
   possible (if not complete); economic variables must be free to
   move, with only one exception: the exchange rate has to become
   the anchor to which all other economic variables are tied.

Those things are essential; everything else is clearly secondary.
(This is an argument against ambitious theoretical models of an
optimal sequencing of reform measures.)

It would be a fatal mistake to attempt to mastermind these processes using a conductor's baton to gradually create a mixture of
half-hearted and, if possible, painless reform elements. Centrally
planned economies had many problems; they had an extremely deep
structural defect, and in the transformation stage we have to start
with the narrowest point (the bottleneck) of the economy. Using
economic terminology, we can say that in this case the marginal
quantities, not the average ones, are decisive.

Using a different logic, we can say that after price liberalization
prices will increase far more than wages, and, therefore, there will
be a rapid fall in real wages; after foreign trade liberalization there
will be a fast decline in the (real) exchange rate. Domestic (or foreign)
critics of liberalization say that real wages are lower than labor
productivity (average productivity) and that the exchange rate is
lower than average purchasing power parity. They are right because
it really is so, but they are wrong when they say that it is a mistake.
The opposite is true. Real wages and the real currency rate have to
be relatively low at this stage because they have to form two cushions

enabling us to bridge a privatization and restructuralization period lasting several years (or a decade). Precisely in the creation of these two cushions is the magic of putting together individual elements of the transformation process.

The faster the privatization, restructuring, and financial stabilization of firms and the faster the creation of a normal microeconomic structure, the shorter the time those two cushions will need to exist. The faster the progress we make with privatization, the smaller will be the cushions needed, and the quicker real wages and real exchange rates will grow.

Hypothetically, those cushions could definitely disappear at the end of the transformation period, not a moment sooner nor a bit later. Eliminating the exchange rate cushion overnight and very quickly emptying the wage cushion (the example of the former German Democratic Republic comes to mind) are possible but immensely expensive—they need the cushion of a richer brother, which the GDR had. Attempting to keep a high exchange rate and high real wages causes instability, inflation, a foreign trade deficit, permanent devaluations, and high unemployment.

This loosely outlined transformation hypothesis will surely be the subject of further, mainly critical, examination by theoreticians, but it also has rich practical implications—for dealing with trade unions, for arguments about protectionism and the so-called social dumping of postcommunist countries, and for the everyday economic policy of the government.

It is a great advantage that we understood many of the rules of the postcommunist era and that we did not let doubters and skeptics influence us and divert us from the only possible path. For this it was necessary to know the rules, to explain them to the citizens of the country (and so gain their support), and to realize the chosen strategy.

12. Privatization Experience: The Czech Case

In the Czech Republic we have been undergoing the most radical and profound systemic transformation in the postcommunist world. We have already crossed the Rubicon dividing the old system and the new one.

Systemic transformation has many aspects, but we consider privatization the most important part of it. We believe that the success of privatization and, therefore, of the whole transformation crucially depends on a clear understanding of the nature, goals, and strategies of privatization. Privatization does not occur in a vacuum; in our case it is part of a very complicated transformation process—from communism to free markets and a free society.

External observers rarely understand the depth and scope of the damage caused by the communist regime. Its destructive effects pervaded politics and the legal system as well as the economy.

Politically, the major victim was an efficient and stable system of political parties. From the point of view of law and justice, the principal victim was a well-defined legal framework and a standard system of government agencies and other institutions enforcing law and order. Economically, we lost a system of well-defined property rights, which forms the basis for the rationality of behavior of economic agents and, therefore, the basis for affluence and prosperity.

The Czechoslovak (and later on the Czech) government constantly stressed its awareness of the complexity of the transformation problem, of its institutional core as well as of its political, legislative, and economic aspects.

Speech delivered at the fourth CEEPN annual conference on "Privatization in Central and Eastern Europe," Ljubljana, Slovenia, December 1993. An earlier version was given at the International Chamber of Commerce meeting, Cancún, Mexico, October 1993.

In the Czech Republic, the early emergence of relatively stable and ideologically well defined political parties is believed to be the most fundamental achievement. With respect to the legal aspects of the whole process, creation of a corresponding system of law and law-enforcing agencies was completed in record time.

In the economic arena, the transformation amounts to nothing more or less than converting central planning into a market economy, which requires deregulation, liberalization, and privatization.

Perestroika versus Transformation

Bearing in mind those points, it must be stressed that it is the economy as a whole, not a particular state-owned enterprise or enterprises, that calls for transformation. In other words, however efficient or inefficient, financially healthy or unhealthy, individual businesses may appear, it is not they but the whole economy that requires a change.

The economy cannot be cured, transformed, or restructured without comprehensive property reform. Without a radical shakeup of property rights, it is unrealistic to expect a positive change in the economy's performance: it will never happen. The perestroika style of economic thinking suggests that the shift from a so-called soft budget constraint to a hard one can be achieved and economic behavior can be modified by rule changes introduced from outside or by macroeconomic measures. That is wrong and misleading. Formal rules and rational macroeconomic policy are a necessary but not a sufficient condition for the desired change.

There is no doubt that it is privatization that distinguishes genuine systemic change from perestroika, and that is what we have been undergoing in the last four years.

Privatization in a Market Economy versus Privatization in a Postcommunist Country

Western countries and some developing countries have also embarked on privatization. The best known privatization in a Western country is probably Margaret Thatcher's in Great Britain in the late 1970s and early 1980s. That kind of privatization represented a partial change in an already existing, properly defined property rights structure.

Unfortunately and surprisingly, it has almost nothing in common with the task we face. The experience accumulated during such a process may be misleading when used in the context of transformation in Central and Eastern Europe. Privatization in our case does not mean the standard shift of property rights between two (or more) well-defined economic agents but the establishment of a property rights structure that was previously either nonexistent or very strange. Privatizing in the West may be viewed as a "reform" process. In the East, however, privatization is the most fundamental objective of a systemic transformation.

Looked at that way, privatization in the postcommunist world is not a process by which property changes hands. Rather, it is the process by which the "nonowner" or quasi-owner, the government, transfers the "nonassets" to their initial owners and by so doing "creates" the "assets." When I say that, I am intentionally not entering a very useful, often neglected debate about the interpretation of the former economic system in our countries.

Lessons We Have Learned

Privatization in a transforming country has some peculiarities that may seem very strange to people better acquainted with the Thatcher type of privatization. All of them suggest special, nonstandard privatization methods.

Privatization Revenues

The government's objective is or should be complete economic transformation rather than maximization of proceeds from the sale of some government assets. Understanding that paradox is not easy, but it is absolutely crucial. (Privatization has, in addition, its own costs, which are not negligible.) That nonstandard goal inevitably calls for nonstandard privatization methods.

Speed of Privatization

Low privatization proceeds are usually believed to be the price paid for speed. On the contrary, we have found that, in the Czech Republic and elsewhere, if there is any correlation between proceeds and time, it is the inverse of what is usually hypothesized for standard privatization. The slower the process, the lower the proceeds of privatization.

One obvious reason is that the true value of the privatized enterprise rapidly decreases due to its unavoidable privatization agony and to the absence of a real owner during the privatization process.

Having understood that, we tried to look for privatization techniques that would be faster than the standard ones. For that reason, we prepared and successfully implemented a nonstandard technique called voucher privatization. The idea is relatively simple. It is based on selling vouchers (quasi-money usable only in the privatization process) to all citizens of the country at a symbolic price. The citizens subsequently use their vouchers to buy shares of privatized firms. (Privatization by voucher turned more than 75 percent of Czech adults into shareholders. Each of them now owns shares in either some of the 1,500 privatized companies or in some of the investment privatization funds.)

Our nonstandard voucher privatization proved to be rapid and efficient. In addition, it facilitated application of standard privatization techniques in the rest of the economy and, in a somewhat indirect manner, sped up their implementation.

The overall privatization program in our country includes not only the voucher scheme but also (1) transfers of state property to municipalities; (2) restitutions to original owners; (3) transformation of Soviet-type cooperatives into cooperatives of real owners; (4) privatization of small-scale business through public auctions; and (5) privatization of medium- and large-scale enterprises through direct sales, joint ventures, tenders, and the like.

Privatization from Below

The efficiency and speed of the privatization process depend heavily on its organization and administration. It is rational to organize privatization in such a way that privatization initiatives are concentrated at the microlevel, not at the government level. Planning, organizational restructuring, dividing, and demonopolizing functions should not be initiated from above by the government. (This approach is thus the exact opposite of what has been done in the former German Democratic Republic.)

Foreign Capital Involvement

In the Czech Republic the presence of foreign investors has always been considered beneficial and, therefore, most welcome. The continuing flow of foreign investment is good proof of our "open arms" policy toward foreign visitors. We are quite happy with the inflow of foreign capital and do not want to accelerate it artificially. It has become one of our fundamental theses that foreign capital will finally enter the country on a massive scale after privatization because the relevant decisions must ultimately depend on the private initiative of real owners rather than on the irresponsible (irresponsible by logic, not by human failure) decisionmaking of government bureaucrats.

Following that philosophy, we resisted strong temptations to introduce a special foreign investment law, under which foreign investors would have received better treatment than domestic ones.

Restructuring of Privatized Enterprises

Privatization is usually initiated to bring efficiency and prosperity to individual privatized enterprises. It is a common myth that privatization in a postcommunist country could and should have the same objectives. What really matters in our case, however, is the effect of privatization on the economy as a whole. Instead of, "Is the enterprise restructured?" the legitimate question is, "Is the economy restructured?" Individual restructuring will have to follow privatization.

The "restructuring problem," widely discussed by experts on standard privatization, is by no means of the same significance in our case as it is in standard privatization. We have no doubt that it is the new owner, not the government, who will find ideas, time, and resources for the necessary restructuring. The Czech government has never listened to advisers who say that its ministries and their agencies should attempt to increase the efficiency of state-owned enterprises before they are privatized.

In the early weeks and months of 1990 when we started to think about privatization, our approach provoked harsh criticism from all imaginable sources. Today, however, even the most prominent international financial organizations have realized that the government of a transforming country is the worst imaginable agent to take care of restructuring tasks and that internationally renowned consulting firms are very expensive and lack country-specific and system-specific knowledge.

It is not an exaggeration to say that we consider it unnecessary to design techniques and legislation with the objective of selecting perfect owners. An objective like that is far beyond the capacity of postcommunist, or any other, governments, and the initial owners may not be the final ones, anyway.

Conclusion

It has been observed—at least in the Czech Republic—that the meaning of privatization may be substantially different in different sociopolitical environments. I am convinced that our approach is correct, and the results demonstrate it. Margaret Thatcher privatized three, four firms a year; we have been privatizing twice that number every day.

13. Creating a Stable Monetary Order

Precondition for Monetary Order

A stable monetary order is for me both a goal and an instrument for achieving other goals. My crucial message is the following: a basic precondition for creating a stable monetary order goes beyond technicalities. To my way of thinking, there is no technical, organizational, or institutional device that could potentially make up for lack of political responsibility—for lack of political and social consensus—in a country that wants to have a stable monetary order. Political and social consensus is a crucial precondition, and I spend most of my time trying to establish and maintain exactly that precondition in my own country.

It seems to me wrong to suggest alternative institutional arrangements, such as currency boards, to compensate for lack of political responsibility or for the inability of politicians to establish and maintain basic support for rational economic policy. I advocate standard institutional arrangements, even if they may not be intellectually challenging. We are not interested in any new social experiments. We lived for 40 years in a traumatic social experiment; that was more than enough. Therefore, we are very conservative.

The Conduct of Monetary Policy

Standard institutional arrangements mean the creation of a two-tiered banking system and the independence of the central bank. As policy prescriptions, I favor rules—rules understood as clear, transparent concepts, not as rigid technical prescriptions. Rational monetary policy needs clearly defined goals and priorities, and there is no more important goal than price stability.

I view monetarism as an inspiration, not as a dogma about technical details. My problem—and it is not mine only—is the question

Address delivered at the Cato Institute's 10th Annual Monetary Conference, Washington, D.C., March 1992.

of how to conduct monetary policy in a situation of extreme fluctuations in economic performance during economic transition. That is a crucial question. All the well-known textbook prescriptions are extremely useful as a basic orientation, but one has to add something to them. At the end of the 1990s, all of us will have perfect time-series data to use in analyzing our mistakes, but we do not have such time-series data now, and we have to act. We have to conduct monetary policy despite the uncertainties we face. There is no simple solution, but I have two suggestions.

First, in the early stage of the transformation process, we must conduct a very restrictive monetary policy. Second, the traumatic decline in production observed during the transition is not a standard depression. Thus, there is no expansionary policy that can cure that decline or prevent unemployment from rising. It is more proper to say that the decline in output is the result of the transformation shakeout, that is, the shakeout of irrational economic activities. The faster such economic activities die, the better.

Very often I have to face arguments in my own country—and, I am very sorry to say, in the West as well—that there is a depression or crisis in Czechoslovakia, Hungary, and Poland and that that crisis requires expansionary economic policies. That is a very dangerous misinterpretation. I have made no optimistic assumptions about the elasticity of the aggregate supply curve of an economy during transition, and I am pretty sure that an expansionary policy would bring inflation and nothing else. The question is when to make a switch to a less restrictive monetary policy. It is quite clear in a country like Czechoslovakia that it must be done after price deregulation. (Today 95 percent of all prices are free to move, which is more than in most West European countries 10 years ago and probably more than in some West European countries even today.) A switch to a less restrictive monetary policy must occur after price deregulation, trade deregulation, and privatization of an important segment of the economy. But this policy is still no real answer.

To my great regret, we do not live in an easy world of homogeneity. We live in a heterogeneous world. We live in a mixed world with a growing private sector that reacts to market signals and a shrinking, but still huge, state-owned sector that does not react to market signals. The state-owned firms are in a state of privatization agony. One of your businessmen recently drew a very good analogy.

He said that state-owned firms in Czechoslovakia behave like they are in a freezer. They are frozen, they do not smell, they do not move, they do not react. We live in a very complicated world, and discovering the proper moment to make monetary policy less restrictive is something we have to do now.

There are some additional analytical issues in the field of monetary policy that are my current headaches. Our basic analytical frame of reference is the quantity theory of money, with its equation of exchange, which says that the quantity of money times the velocity of circulation of money equals the price level times the volume of transactions. We think in terms of those four variables and implicitly use them to analyze our economic situation, our economic policy.

The Unreliability of Official Data

The problem of the unreliability of data on prices and output is well known. Under the old system, economic data favored the communist regime. During the transition to a market economy, however, the official statistical data help to discredit reform efforts. Because there are many unreported economic activities in the mushrooming private sector, statistical offices are unable to analyze and take into consideration all the economic data. In my country, the official data really fail to show the fluctuations in output due to the privatization of small-scale businesses. For example, our statistical office publishes retail trade data only for firms with more than 100 employees. In November 1991 retail trade for those firms had declined by some 35 percent. While such information would be extremely relevant for any standard and stable economy, and especially for a centrally planned economy where all retail firms have more than 100 employees, it is now absolutely irrelevant. Nevertheless, the decline in that measure of retail trade made the headlines in Czechoslovakia and in the *New York Times* as well. The unreliability of data on prices and quantities is, therefore, a crucial issue.

Is Monetary Policy Overly Restrictive?

But that is not the main problem we face. I am afraid that our monetary policy may be too restrictive. My hypothesis is that in a country moving from a centrally planned economy to a market economy, transactions grow much faster than current output. So if monetary policy focuses on increasing the money supply in line with current output, monetary policy will be overly restrictive. For that reason, I have some doubts about our monetary policy.

There may be at least three reasons that transactions grow faster than output. The first is that in the past we had only current output transactions, whereas in the transformation period we have huge property transfers. The differences between current output transactions and property transactions are large in a newly emerging market economy. Therefore, a simple quantity of money equation, which relies on current output, will underestimate the demand for money. That is a serious concern.

Second, in the world of central planning we had only real transactions, payments for the delivery of goods and services. There was no financial sector. However, in the transition to a market system, financial transactions become important and add to the demand for money.

Finally, there is another important reason for a dramatic increase in transactions in economies making the transition to a market system, namely, the enormous multiplication of the number of economic agents as markets widen. In the past, economic transactions were very often done administratively inside large enterprises without the intermediation of money. But today there are many new economic agents and numerous exchanges among thousands of firms instead of movements of goods inside large firms. That institutional change is another reason for the enormous increase in the demand for money and helps to explain why it is so difficult to measure that demand.

Monetary policy may also be overly restrictive because of the conservative nature of our commercial banks. At present, we have two different patterns of commercial-bank behavior in Central Europe. We have the behavior of commercial banks in countries like Poland and in the former Soviet Union, where the situation is such that commercial banks grant credit very easily. And we have the behavior of commercial banks in Czechoslovakia, where the newly born independent banks try to play a very conservative role and are probably overcautious. The difference probably reflects the different mentalities in various countries of Eastern and Central Europe. We were always overcautious in the past in Czechoslovakia, and the overly conservative behavior of our commercial banks creates an additional problem that we have to solve. There is no reason to try to force the banks to grant more credit, but we are afraid that maybe they are too risk averse.

Other Issues in Creating a Monetary Order

There are three final issues, which I will mention briefly. First, there is the issue of whether one country should try to enter the global economy alone or try to organize a regional monetary arrangement as a way to integrate itself into the global economy. My answer is straightforward. There is no reason to create sophisticated, complicated, and artificial monetary arrangements. Creating, as I like to call them, "poor men's clubs" is a sure way to block our fast entry into the world economy.

The second issue is whether we should keep restricting currency convertibility to current account convertibility or jump immediately into the world of capital account convertibility. I have nothing against full convertibility, but for practical reasons it seems that current account convertibility is sufficient for us now. It is sufficient because it opens the country to the rest of the world. We do not intend to centrally plan the introduction of competition at home. For us the best way to liquidate domestic monopolies is to introduce international competition, and that is exactly what current account convertibility accomplishes.

The third issue is whether to have fixed or flexible exchange rates. I was horrified at the very beginning by the idea of having fixed exchange rates. I remember that the International Monetary Fund was shocked when I suggested a flexible exchange-rate regime. I was really afraid that announcing a fixed, highly devalued exchange rate three days before the introduction of price liberalization could create a vicious inflationary spiral. I wanted to let the exchange rate be free to move for some time and maybe only then introduce a fixed exchange rate. I am glad that I was wrong. Nothing happened as a result of the announcement of the fixed exchange rate, and it seems to me that using the exchange rate as an anchor for all other monetary variables in the economy is a good policy.

14. Adam Smith's Legacy and Economic Transformation

It is most intellectually stimulating for me to have this opportunity to speak of the influence of the ideas of Adam Smith, the founding father of economic science, on the thinking that has guided Czechoslovakia's economic transformation.

Czechoslovakia and other communist countries suffered for many decades under an inefficient centrally planned and centrally administered system. It was a wasteful system, a system not reflective of human wants and desires. It is not necessary to try to add anything new to the criticism of such a system; the task today is to replace that system with a smoothly functioning, efficient market economy based on private property and private initiative.

Such a system works best under a small government and should be fully integrated into the world economy. In that respect, Adam Smith's message is crucial and very relevant. My experience tells me that a real understanding or lack of understanding of Smith's message is what distinguishes the successful from the unsuccessful transformation of postcommunist countries.

Visions and Reform Strategies

I am convinced that Adam Smith supplies us with a vision of where to go that needs no correction. A laissez-faire, market economy (as I always say, without any qualifying, or perhaps disqualifying, adjectives), small government, liberty, and responsibility are the catchwords of our thinking. That may be trivial to you, but it is not trivial in our part of the world. We live in a world where the concepts of entrepreneurship and business were dangerous to advocate and even unknown.

Adam Smith Address delivered to the National Association of Business Economists, Dallas, Texas, September 1992.

Smith teaches us that the role of an entrepreneur is crucial, that to follow one's own interest is the best and the only available way to maximize the welfare of all members of society. In the past we tried to invent and introduce utopian motives for human action, whereas Smith knew that for the smooth, efficient functioning of an economic and social system we have to make use of "the strongest, rather than the highest" motives of human behavior. That idea was heresy in 18th-century England and is heresy now in the contemporary postcommunist world. Smith explained to us that the strongest motive is "the uniform, constant and uninterrupted effort of every man to better his conditions." He knew as well that the wealth of a nation grows only when individuals are getting richer.

All of that is of utmost importance in our part of the world just now because there are still people who dream of a paternalistic state and who have open or hidden suspicions that anyone who gets richer does so at the expense of somebody else and that the creation of wealth is a zero-sum game.

Smith's message is important not only in the rather esoteric world of ideas and visions. I am convinced that he—at least implicitly—also gives us clear instructions regarding an overall reform strategy. That is a very pragmatic issue.

Smith knew that the market and its evolution are a spontaneous process that cannot be planned, organized, or constructed, because they are the outcome of millions of individual human actions, not of an ambitious single act based on constructivist human design (to use the famous dictum of Hayek).

We are, in our part of the world, under pressure to create markets first and to "use" them after that. Everybody (especially our opponents) wants to see perfect reform blueprints for a detailed sequencing of individual reform measures first. They do not want to actively participate in the often difficult and traumatic transformation process. They used to think in terms of "building socialism," and now they want to "build" markets. They want, therefore, to introduce the invisible hand of the market by means of the visible and omnipotent hand of a government bureaucrat. Smith's message is, however, clear: we have to liberalize, deregulate, and privatize at a very early stage of reform, even if we will be confronted with rather weak and, therefore, not fully efficient markets. The very fashionable and sophisticated debate about optimal sequencing of reform measures and about shock therapy versus gradualism is simply missing the point.

We must, whether we like it or not, proceed with many parallel steps without trying to mastermind the whole process. Waiting for optimal sequencing means postponing reform into the distant future, preserving the existing irrational and unstable state of affairs, and falling into the reform trap that brings about economic collapse and a total disintegration of society.

Recent Czechoslovak Experience

To switch to a more optimistic note, let's turn to Czechoslovakia. I would argue that we understood Adam Smith's message and in the past almost three years have been trying to follow it. We have

- a clear, strong vision of where to go, and the politicians and political parties are prepared to defend it;
- a pragmatic, flexible reform strategy based on nonambitious government intervention;
- a basic political and social consensus on reform that was—at least in the Czech lands—confirmed in the 1992 elections (a phenomenon that has not yet occurred in any other postcommunist country);
- the first positive and undoubtedly promising results of price stability, currency convertibility, deregulation, and privatization and the ability and willingness to survive and accept the drastic economic shakeout and accompanying decline in output that occurs when artificially created (and maintained) demand both at home and abroad simply disappears overnight.

I am deeply convinced that the reform process—after price liberalization, after integration into the world economy by means of foreign trade liberalization, after introduction of internal currency convertibility, and after initiation of a vigorous privatization program—begins to have its own internal dynamic and can only be stopped by huge mistakes.

We are well aware of the fact that special attention must be devoted to the maintenance of price stability, which we consider a precondition for everything else. If there is any lesson I have learned during the past three years, it is to stick with my long-term belief in pursuing cautious, restrictive monetary and fiscal policies and not following the arguments of various irresponsible expansionists who would like to artificially speed up the economy by pouring money into it— by either printing money or deficit financing.

The role of foreign participation in our transformation process is significant but somewhat different than is usually thought. We do *not* desperately need

- foreign aid (in the form in which it has been given to developing countries in the past);
- debt cancellation (as is suggested for some other postcommunist countries);
- technical assistance and consulting in the forms we know;
- loans from international development lending institutions to support dubious government projects, sectoral or regional policies, huge infrastructure projects, and the like;
- trade barriers and restrictions.

We do need, however, and we do need desperately

- access to world markets and the end of protectionist practices in individual countries and in various regional blocks;
- foreign real investments;
- macroeconomic stand-by arrangements facilitating price deregulation, foreign trade liberalization, and currency convertibility in countries with limited hard currency reserves and huge currency debts.

Conclusion

Despite the first positive results of economic transformation, former communist countries still face tremendous problems and have a long way to go. We need positive externalities. The lighthouse is a standard textbook example of a positive externality. We have the lighthouse of Adam Smith's teaching, and we will heed its beam.

PART III

THE CZECH REPUBLIC IN EUROPE

15. Notes on Europe

Discussing Europe in the middle of 1994, we should not be put on the defensive by accepting as our starting point pessimistic headlines in the media or various catastrophic scenarios suggested by those who tend to see the world as a playground for their own ambitious, constructivist "human designs" they would like to enforce upon us. We should start with an unbiased and unprejudiced analysis, proceed to the identification of real (as opposed to fictitious) problems, and end up with feasible suggestions for their solution.

Where Are We Now?

Looking at our continent without rose-colored glasses and with sharp analytical eyes, we should not forget that Europe today is less than five years past the "Velvet Revolutions" in its important central and eastern parts, less than five years past the unplanned and even unexpected collapse of communism and the demolition of the Iron Curtain, less than five years past the dismantling of COMECON (the Council for Mutual Economic Assistance) and the Warsaw Pact. We have to appreciate that because of that historic event—or, maybe, in spite of it—Europe has undoubtedly become more free, more democratic, less dangerous, more open, more integrated, more united, less ideological, and more pragmatic than at any time in the memory of living Europeans.

The Central and East European countries clearly differ in the degree of their success at overcoming the communist heritage and creating the institutions of a free society and a market economy, though it should be admitted that their progress is surprisingly fast and generally positive. Critics who disagree with that assessment seem to have forgotten their past condemnation of communism.

Originally published as "Economic and Political Changes in Europe," *The Economist*, September 10, 1994.

Communism would not have been so evil, so inhuman, so oppressive, so irrational, so ineffective, had it been possible to create a normally functioning society and economy in a couple of months or years without undergoing a profound and painful political, social, and economic transformation, which has a nonzero time dimension and cannot, therefore, be accomplished in a shock-therapy, overnight way.

The success of the transition seems undeniable to me, and the postcommunist European countries have demonstrated that they are no less European than their neighbors who happened not to live through the communist trauma. The countries in transition understood very quickly that the inevitable systemic change (not just perestroika) is a domestic task and that the contribution of the rest of the world is marginal at best. The only country that is going through transition with massive external help, the former German Democratic Republic, has probably more, definitely not fewer, problems than any other postcommunist country.

We all know that the overall success of transformation is marred by one important and disturbing failure—the Yugoslav crisis. However, it is, for me at least, difficult to accept the implicit assumption that Sarajevo is a typical case of the postcommunist syndrome, which is due to develop in every similar country and therefore endangers the whole of Europe. The tragedy did not occur in the most "communist," most totalitarian, most undemocratic country; it did not occur in a country whose borders had been totally closed in the past decades; it did not occur in a country that had been under complete Soviet hegemony. The splitting of Yugoslavia was not part of an almost standard "velvet" revolutionary process, and it should be mentioned that it became more tragic than similar events in some non-European parts of the former Soviet Union.

People who accepted the interpretation that something like Sarajevo is a typical postcommunist phenomenon should have looked for another real Sarajevo in another country. It is much more appropriate to take it as an exceptional event and a unique phenomenon. The latter interpretation does not force us to form new, additional, totally unnecessary institutions to safeguard peace and stability in Europe (as is often suggested in the Western part of Europe). I have repeatedly tried to caution West Europeans against wearing Sarajevo glasses or using Sarajevo optics, because doing so blocks the normal evolution of European relations and institutions. It would be the same mistake to demonize Russia, expect her to behave irrationally, disregard her internal stabilizing instincts and her ability to "muddle through."

Western Europe is moving to a deeper form of formal integration than this continent has ever experienced. The fact that the form and pace of the integration process more or less reflect real, genuine interests of the European citizens and the European countries, rather than constructivist blueprints approved at various European summits, and the fact that the process is therefore dictated more by "human action than by human design" (to use Hayek's famous dictum) is not surprising, should be welcome, and should not inspire nervousness or doomsday scenarios and forecasts. The barriers between countries are—in spite of the bureaucrats', lobbyists', and rent seekers' resistance—getting smaller, and that undoubtedly brings more freedom and well-being to all Europeans (especially the members of the European Union). That process should continue, and I do not see any potentially disturbing factors that would hinder its continuation in the foreseeable future.

The concept of integration (elimination of barriers to the movement of people, ideas, goods and services, labor and capital) does not, however, imply the prefabrication of all Europeans into a special breed of *Homo sapiens* to be called *Homo europeus*. I believe that integration—defined as a process of gradual elimination of all restrictions on the interplay of human beings in all dimensions of life—enjoys widespread support in Europe but that the desire for unification, which I have to understand as integration plus an additional vision of the structure and organization of human society, is not so easily shared by all Europeans and definitely represents a different and more ambitious goal. The use of labels such as Euro-skeptics and Euro-optimists (or Eurorealists and Euroidealists) could be misleading if we do not define clearly what we are talking about. I am a Euro-optimist as regards the future as well as the overall positive impact of European integration and a Eurorealist as regards our ability (not to speak of the necessity) to unify Europe under one ideological banner. But, generally speaking, there is no need for pessimism or skepticism about the dynamics of the essentially positive evolutionary path toward integration.

Nevertheless, both Eastern and Western Europe have real problems, which should not be underestimated.

The Challenges of Transition

The most important task for the Central and East European countries is to succeed in the ongoing transformation process, not to fall into the dangerous reform trap of half measures and useless political and social concessions, and not to give up the fight against an already emerging "reform fatigue." The reform politicians must be able to

- formulate a clear, transparent vision of a promising and realizable future;
- explain that vision to the citizens of their countries and defend it against populists of all political and ideological shades;
- implement a consistent reform strategy and introduce unpopular and painful reform measures exactly at the moment when they must be introduced rather than try to satisfy vocal rent-seeking and lobbying groups, which fight for maximization of their own short-term advantages to the detriment of the whole of society.

The reform politicians have to take into consideration—with all of its implications—the fact that the radical transformation of the whole societal system is a multidimensional social process (with its own dynamic) and not an exercise in applied economics, sociology, or political science. The people involved in such a radical societal change are not passive objects but human beings with their own dreams, habits, preferences, and priorities. They must get a chance, political as well as economic. A standard system of political parties has to be created, because it is the only mechanism that can guarantee the formation of a basic political and social consensus on the transformation vision, strategy, and results. Privatizing, deregulating, and liberalizing—in conditions of sufficient macroeconomic stability—are the order of the day.

Most of the postcommunist countries have already introduced the first set of reform measures. Some of them have done so with hesitations, some inconsistently, and some unfortunately have not gathered the necessary "critical mass" of system-changing measures. Therefore, they have not been able to achieve a fundamental, qualitative systemic change and score the first tangible results. We see that the initial euphoria has evaporated and the original nationwide unity (which existed only in a negative sense) has been lost. In some countries that results in an enormous degree of political atomization and could lead to increasing political instability. That is a real Central and East European and, because of that, all-European problem, whose solution cannot be, as I already mentioned, imported from outside. That problem has to be solved where it exists.

West European Issues

The West European countries face another challenge. The collapse of Soviet-style communism (or socialism) shifted the eternal human question of how much free, responsible individuals should be regulated and controlled from a simple dilemma to a much more complicated one. The totalitarian practices of communism and its irrational, state-owned (which means without real owners) and centrally planned economy are easy to criticize and to refute. It is more difficult, however, to find an optimal equilibrium point in the real world between the freedom of individuals and regulation by the state (not to mention supranational institutions).

By all available evidence, Western Europe is not in an optimal position in this respect. The prevailing system is too heavy because of overregulation and overcontrol; too socialist because of generous welfare state transfer payments, which are unconnected to any achievement and undermine elementary work ethics and individual responsibility; too closed because of the high degree of protectionism; too slow because of bureaucratic and administrative procedures; and too costly because of all of those things. I do not pretend to reveal anything new and analytically unknown here, but it is fair to say that the Thatcherite (anti-Keynesian, liberal) revolution stopped halfway and is yet to be completed.

Several visible manifestations of that are worth mentioning. First, there is the economically high, unproductive (and politically and socially explosive) unemployment rate, which seems to be resistant to varying rates of economic growth and the business cycle. It has been brought about neither by an excessive supply of labor nor by lack of demand for labor, neither by immigration nor by lack of technological progress, neither by excessive imports of Southeast Asian products nor by cheap labor in Eastern Europe. The most relevant factor, which explains the whole problem, is the excessive domestic wage rate (vis-à-vis the productivity of labor). False solutions—such as the fashionable cuts of working hours—are missing the point. Wages are high for two main reasons: the wage rate in a narrow sense is high because it loses its microeconomic foundations at the level of the firm and is determined at a macrolevel between the state and labor organizations (trade unions), and, in addition, mandatory costs, imposed by nonliberal legislation, push wages even further up. Put simply, Europeans have to reconcile rewards with achievements; otherwise, some of them will be out of work forever.

Second, various European countries have reached the limit of their state budget deficits (an extreme case is Sweden). The expenditure side of the budget has a built-in expansionary tendency, taxes cannot be further increased, and to move backward along the Laffer curve seems to be politically too dangerous. Budget deficits, as an unpleasant Keynesian relic, are connected with the logic and structure of the European welfare state. That is not accidental fiscal mismanagement (by an irresponsible minister of finance). It is deeply rooted in contemporary European society and is based on a misplaced emphasis on redistributive instead of productive processes by a significant number of European politicians (and their constituencies).

Third, people in some countries are dissatisfied with their politicians (who tend to maximize their number of years in office instead of offering bold political initiatives) and are voting for new faces. That is reflected in the emergence of new, nontraditional political parties. It is, in my opinion, wrongly interpreted as the end of ideologically well defined political parties and the end of ideology (in the sense of Fukuyama). Nothing is further from the truth. The ideological dispute is here to stay, is subtler but no less important, and we should be aware of that.

These are real West European and therefore all-European problems whose solutions must be found before the end of the century. It seems to me that none of the problems just mentioned is connected with the small size of a typical European country or with the need to shift the solution to a supranational entity. We cannot, therefore, escape our responsibility for solving them at home, where they have arisen.

Summing Up

The collapse of communism helped the whole of Europe, not just its eastern part. Western Europe may continue to exist geographically, but it has more or less disappeared politically. European institutions should not artificially divide Europe into two parts, the luckier one and the less lucky one (as in the days of the Cold War); they should, rather, create an umbrella for all the democratic European countries that want to be an active part of an old but free, diverse, peaceful, and efficient continent.

16. Europe: Our Visions and Our Strategies

European countries share many things, but Europe is based on an undeniable diversity, which makes for a very fragile balance. We take it for granted that existing differences, habits, dreams, attitudes, and interests cannot and should not be suppressed, because European countries provide natural frames of reference for our lives. Europe is, nevertheless, more than the sum of its parts and deserves our protection. Its existence makes us richer both materially and spiritually; it is our duty to take advantage of all the potential synergistic effects.

It must be fascinating to be aware of that and to be in the Council of Europe and feel the enormous responsibility of making decisions that concern the entire Continent.

As prime minister of the Czech Republic in these stormy, turbulent, demanding but also exciting times of historic political, social, and economic transformation, I would like to outline some of the assumptions on which the Czech view of European integration is based.

The Czech Republic is located in the heart of Europe, has always been part of Europe, and after decades of seclusion and isolation wants once again to actively participate in European affairs.

We interpret our "Europeanism" as an obligation to safeguard and preserve our distinctive features because we believe they are exactly what we can offer to Europe, to all of you. To deserve its name, Europe must apply the principles of exchange and equivalence; we all have to give and to take. Should there be nothing to give, there would be nothing to take, either, and we would be part of a debilitating, zero-sum game.

Speech delivered to the Parliamentary Assembly of the Council of Europe, Strasbourg, January 30, 1995.

The communist regime in our country is definitely over, and our unfortunate experience made us especially sensitive to all kinds of deficiencies, disturbances, and violations of freedom, which occur even in countries where democratic regimes have prevailed for decades or centuries.

Our approach to European institutions is based more on the ideas of openness; freedom; exchange; and voluntary, spontaneous activities than on the ideas of constructivism, statism, interventionism, regulation, and control. We believe more in "human action" than in "human design" and are convinced that that simple truth is relevant to both domestic and international affairs.

We believe in Europe because it is genuinely attractive to us. We are convinced that Europe is here (and here to stay) and that Europe is very real. Some of our citizens are, nevertheless, confused because they cannot see it or touch it. Therefore, they suggest building institutions. But we are not sure that Europe should aim for that kind of tangibility.

We do not think Europe should be stronger or bigger to be able to compete with the United States or Japan because we do not believe in bigness. We know that the well-known law of increasing returns to scale is counterbalanced in reality by the effect of other, no less important, laws—the limits of organizational or administrative efficiency, knowledge that is inevitably dispersed among individuals, and the impossibility of its aggregation by means of available information technology. We do not believe that technical progress needs huge continents controlled from single places. On the contrary, we know that technical progress needs creativity, motivation, and openness and the elimination of all man-made restrictions, impediments, and fences.

Since our Velvet Revolution in November 1989, we have accumulated some relevant experience with a historically unique process called transformation—a systemic change from the political and economic structures of communism to a free society and a market economy.

Let me use that perspective for a brief discussion of two seemingly unrelated but intrinsically (and structurally) similar issues: the logic and characteristics of transition from communism to a free society and the logic and characteristics of the evolution of European integration, especially the European Union. I will not go into details; I will only outline two essential preconditions for successfully accomplishing both tasks.

What we need is a clear, strong, transparent, and appealing vision of what we really want. When we talk about our Czech transition, our vision is straightforward. We want a free society, based on a system of pluralistic parliamentary democracy and a market economy (without adjectives).

Freedom is based on the permanent contest of competing ideas, not on the dominance of any one of them. The value of freedom itself is crucial because it is more general and more encompassing than the value of any one specific ideology, ambition, or special interest. Problems arise whenever or wherever another objective is put ahead of it—irrespective of the well-meant intentions and purposes of individuals who suggest or advocate other objectives. The typical conflict in our part of the world these days stems from efforts to attribute higher values to different visions and objectives. The vision of a good or moral society is the standard case because its advocates believe that free society does not always produce results we and they like. The definition of goodness or morality they have in mind is, however, rather vague, and what is more important is that freedom can be "introduced," whereas goodness and morality can be only preached or disseminated by giving advice or setting a good example. Guaranteeing freedom is one of the crucial tasks of the ongoing systemic change; indeed, it is the main task for those who organize that change. Preaching morality is an individual task for those who feel entitled to do so. Such activity deserves our admiration, but it cannot be a definitional feature of any society and, therefore, it cannot be part of a transformation vision.

When we talk about the process of European integration, our vision need not be less straightforward and must be related to our societal vision. We want a free Europe; we want European institutions that would enhance the freedom of individuals living in Europe; we want institutions that would make our lives happier and that would contribute to the increased welfare of all of us. We do not want institutions that would try to control us, regulate us, coordinate us, organize us, prefabricate us; institutions that would try to force their own values, ambitions, or prejudices on us; institutions that would favor special interests at the cost of the interests of the whole.

A strict distinction between goals and means is another crucial part of our vision. European institutions are no more than an instrument; they are not a goal in themselves and must be evaluated with that distinction in mind. They must be strictly instrumental and should never become substitutes for real goals. That may sound trivial, but it is not.

The vision must be supplemented by a feasible strategy for achieving it. I do not intend to discuss the technicalities of the most suitable strategy, the comparative advantages of gradualism and shock therapy, optimal sequencing rules, or various aspects of often-neglected cost-benefit analyses.

A successful strategy must be based on a symmetrical and balanced interplay of political, social, and economic measures. To omit one of them is the fastest way to failure. The strategy to be applied

- must be technically, administratively, and organizationally feasible;
- must be "fair"; its costs and benefits must be widespread, and its impacts should not exceed the tolerance limit of various social groups;
- must gain and keep credibility and must be adequately explained to the whole society.

When we look back at the recent transformation attempts in postcommunist Europe, we can see many troubles connected with inconsistent visions, infeasible strategies, and huge gaps between winners and losers, but the main troubles are connected with the lack of credibility of politicians and their programs as well as the lack of social consensus among the citizens of the transforming countries.

If there is a bottleneck in the transformation, it is the inability to secure sufficient political support for the necessary transformation measures. One government after another has had to face a growing opposition because it is easier to promote a negative political program than a positive one. The Czech Republic has so far been successful in that respect, and I hope it will continue to be.

The present European issue—the evolution of European institutions, the substance of the European integration process—constitutes a similar problem. It needs both a vision and a strategy, a strategy that is feasible, fair, and credible. To formulate a European vision is not easy.

The original vision—prevention of a replay of the disastrous Second World War, to integrate Germany into Europe in a new way, to promote the values of freedom and democracy against the communist ideology, to promote welfare by removing trade barriers and by creating a common market—was more or less accepted by most Europeans. That vision has been quietly replaced by a more comprehensive vision—Europeanism, more coordination from a single place, more uniformity in policy, common policies in many fields, belief in extensive regulation, reduction of the authority and responsibility of nation-states (or historic states), efforts to create a European identity, and the like. I think such a vision still has to be explained to many Europeans; their questions must be answered, and their doubts must be dispelled.

The strategies face familiar problems—the sequencing issue, the gradualism or shock-therapy dilemma, distributional difficulties, credibility, and so on. Those are not trivial problems because they affect millions of human beings with their dreams, habits, and prejudices. Again, credibility is most important.

I do not believe that the process of European integration should be based on

- expectations that European feelings will be stronger than those of national identity on the part of most Europeans;
- a shift of the fragile balance of "unity in diversity" toward more unity than diversity;
- ambitions to create a strong, unified, and united entity able to compete with the United States and Japan;
- temporary fashions in ideology, demonstrated in the current approaches to industrial policy, trade policy, social charter, and environmental aspirations.

The process of European integration should be based on undisputed ideas and approaches:

- the natural affinity of most Europeans for Europe,
- similar cultures and histories,
- genuine common interests, and
- geographical proximity.

Practically speaking, we have to define "public goods at the European level" with the implicit assumption that all other things are either private goods or public goods at the national (or lower) level. We do not believe in extending the domain of public goods and are convinced that most of them can be supplied at the national level. A discussion based on analysis, not on emotions, is long overdue. We are ready to take a very active part in it.

To conclude, I would like to assure you that the Czech Republic—now in its early post-transformation stage—will complete its historic systemic change very soon and will be a democratic, peaceful, stable country and a reliable partner to all of you.

We are true Europeans; despite all our questions, doubts, and occasional objections, we want to actively participate in the process of European integration and to become a full member of the European Union as soon as possible.

17. The Nation-State as a Building Block of European Integration

I hope my positivist approach to today's topic complements the normative thinking that prevails in studies of law and government both here and elsewhere.

Thinking about, and particularly operating or functioning in, the rather tricky space between supranationalism and regionalism is not abstract theorizing for me. The need to resolve that issue and to search for the most reasonable integration into European political, economic, and security structures has become an integral part of everyday life in this country and in this part of the Continent. In that respect, we are no theoreticians; we are authentic practitioners. From that special perspective, I would like to raise a few points that may be of some interest to you.

My simple but, I insist, nontrivial starting point is that neither the term "region" nor the term "state" (or "nation-state") nor the term "supranational integration" should be understood as containing a value judgment. They should not be taken as value-loaded terms; there is nothing a priori positive or negative about any one of them; and none of them should be considered a goal in itself. In accord with my principal ideological beliefs, I have to stress that the basic entity of any democratic society is the individual human being, not any institution. The decisive criterion for evaluating all possible kinds and forms of human institutions or organizations (collectivities) is, therefore, their positive or negative contribution to the maximization of the well-being or happiness of individual members of that collectivity—not the other way around. The individual has the primary position; any collectivity's position is, therefore, secondary because all collectivities are only derivatives.

Speech delivered at the Zavikon conference on "Between Supranationalism and Regionalism," Dräger Foundation, Prague, June 10, 1994.

That is not an irrelevant or impractical ideological statement. It is, in my opinion, extremely important for our discussion. The never-ending attempts to defend regionalism on the basis of an a priori positive "value" hidden in so-called self-governance; to defend nation-states with arguments of cheap and aggressive nationalism; or to defend supranationalism using cosmopolitan, anti-nationalistic arguments is wrong, misleading, and in many respects even danger-ous. Those positions may very easily lead us toward acceptance of some dubious normative visions or theories and toward a world where only one of those "truths" is allowed. We have spent much of our lives in such a world and are, therefore, very sensitive in this respect—more so than our Western friends.

Our point of departure is, therefore, much different. We pragmati-cally suggest analyzing and evaluating alternative institutional arrangements using two simple and transparent criteria: their effi-ciency and their feasibility.

Their efficiency depends on the relative costs and benefits they provide for their members (or participants), and their feasibility depends on their authenticity, on the willingness of their members to associate in them on a voluntary basis and in a constructive manner. I would like to say a few words about both aspects of such an evaluation.

When talking about integration of human beings into territorially defined "collectivities," I am afraid the discussants use two a priori and, for those of us who do not think in Orwellian doublethink, contradictory arguments. When talking about regions of a country, they repeat the seductive catch phrase "small is beautiful"; when they talk about conglomerates of countries, they reveal their subcon-scious phobia of "the American challenge" (or the Japanese or Islamic challenge) by stressing the need for bigness, for strength, for positive returns to scale, and the like. In both cases they are wrong. The costs and benefits of various human activities and of different forms and sizes of organizations are nonlinear, nonhomog-eneous, noncontinuous. Comparing them requires an impartial and unbiased approach. I see such an approach neither at home nor in the rest of Europe these days.

That is one problem that bothers me. Another one is my frustration with facing again and again a strange technocratic or "neutralistic" approach to human organizations, as if we were talking about labora-tory experiments and not about social institutions reflecting human behavior, which is undoubtedly based on a mixture of power instincts, ideology, and vested interests. Serious arguments should be based on assumptions about human behavior as well as on assumptions about inclinations or propensities of various—small or large—institutions to intervene, impose constructivist regulations, and so on. I will not try to suggest such arguments here today, but they must be seriously discussed.

Feasibility is, in my understanding, connected with the acceptance or nonacceptance of an institution as such by its members or, to put it differently, with identity. I do not want to argue that new organizations can never be created, that people are backward looking only, that they are absolutely unable to get rid of their past and to start anew. However, it is possible to make changes if and only if there is no strong identity of people with another, competing collectivity; the old source of identity is discredited; and the new one is expected and welcome.

In the Czech Republic there has not been—in a long, long time, if ever—a strong, genuine regional identity, and I doubt that the new fashionable (among leftist intellectuals) regionalistic idea, based on civil society or self-governance, is strong enough to be taken seriously. Ideas of a community (not of communitarianism) and of a nation-state (not of nationalism or statism) are much stronger and much more authentic.

Similarly, I do not believe the idea of Europe (in a political, not a geographic, sense) is sufficiently strong to compete successfully with the idea of a nation-state (or with a historical state), and I do not believe the idea of the nation has been discredited.

To suggest or to assume that Sarajevo or Bosnia helped to discredit the nation is at best a tremendous simplification. Sarajevo and Bosnia, on the contrary, demonstrate that the idea of a nation is not dead and that to suppress it artificially (as Tito did after World War II) paradoxically creates, not rules out, such a horrible state of affairs as we witness in the former Yugoslavia just now. The success of a European integration movement, therefore, depends on the emergence of strong feelings of identity, not on their neglect or on somebody's wishful thinking.

My conclusion is that European integration should be based on nation-states (or historical states) as its building blocks because only that will pave the way to a smooth, friendly, and efficient functioning of the whole Continent. The beneficiaries will be us, Europeans.

18. The Czech Republic and Its Integration into European Political, Security, and Economic Structures

I would like to begin by stressing my basic assumption that our country is and has always been part of Europe. Because we do not want to be deprived of advantages stemming from membership in European institutions, we want to become a member as early as possible. The comments that follow do not contradict that introductory declaration.

In some respects our approach was summarized four years ago, immediately after the Velvet Revolution, in the slogan "Back to Europe." At that crucial moment of our history, we strongly resisted suggestions of some of our Western friends that we create a special, subregional institution in Central and Eastern Europe because it would have divided us from Europe. Even the term "Visegrad countries"—used more often abroad than here to refer to the Czech Republic, Slovakia, Hungary, and Poland—had and has a very limited meaning for those of us who spent 40 years under an inefficient and oppressive communist regime and in a debilitating economic integration called COMECON (Council for Mutual Economic Assistance), not to mention the Warsaw Pact. We share the same European values as our Western neighbors, and we share the same belief in the importance as well as the positive impact of European integration processes. That belief is an undisputable and undisputed, therefore natural, starting point of Czech foreign policy. That is what I take for granted.

Our debate is more or less about forms of European integration, and at that level I intend to make several points. When we say that we are ready to participate in a reasonable European integration, it

---

Address delivered to the conference on "Europe and Us," organized by the Patriae Foundation, Prague, May 1994.

105

does not imply that we are in favor of a complete and unconditional European unification.

There are at least three basic reasons for my stressing so much and so often the difference between Europe and European institutions as well as the difference between integration and unification.

Identity

The communist regime was not easy to live under, and its collapse is not without long-term consequences. We are trying to overcome its effects as fast as possible, and I am convinced that the Czech Republic has already reached what I call the early post-transformation stage. The main transformation tasks have been accomplished:

- We have created a standard system of political parties, which function in a pluralistic, parliamentary democracy.
- We are maintaining the national political and social consensus on transformation goals, strategies, and results.
- We have formed a market economy (without adjectives) and realized rapid privatization, macroeconomic stabilization, and widespread and radical liberalization and deregulation.

In the communist era we were oppressed both individually and nationally. Under the banners of proletarian internationalism we lost our national (and state) identity, and we are now in the process of redefining it, in the process of reformulating our state and national interests. All of that has its historical dimension. Most Central and East European countries jumped (or fell) into the communist regime more or less directly after the collapse of three, essentially supranational, empires (the Austrian, the Ottoman, and the Russian ones). The postcommunist countries, therefore, face a double task today: finding their own identities and not losing them straightaway on the road to Europe. Because of that dual and difficult task, I prefer the idea of "integration" of European states (and nations) to the idea of "unification" of European citizens in a federalist state.

Ideology

The problem has its ideological dimension as well. I am deeply convinced that the success of all of us in Europe, not the success of Europe, depends on the quality and structure of the prevailing political, social, and economic systems and not on the existence, scope, and activities of multilateral European institutions. The success of all of us depends on the degree of freedom we have: on the degree of freedom of markets and trade, on our ability to get rid of unnecessary government intervention introduced in the past in the name of aggressive socialism (or communism) in one part of Europe or of the welfare state (a milder form of socialism) in another, on our ability to get rid of various forms of bureaucratic manipulation, on our determination to suppress the powerful social-welfare-endangering lobbying and rent-seeking groups, on our capacity to put economic fundamentals in order.

The original ideas about the current version of European integration in the late 1940s and early 1950s were necessarily based on the ideological paradigm of the first part of the 20th century. That period was characterized by a general loss of faith in the positive outcome of unorganized coordination or cooperation of individual microsubjects. There were, therefore, many advocates of the idea of some sort of worldwide or Continentwide dirigisme in an effort to complement bureaucratic state intervention at the national level.

Today most of us have a totally different perception of the world, and it must (very often against vested interests of European bureaucrats) sooner or later find its expression in the forms of the European integration process. The more belief in free markets and free trade we have, the less belief we have in ambitious political engineering and in bureaucratic intervention and the more we favor a looser concept of integration over a tighter concept of union.

Nationalism

Finally, the whole idea of Europe should not be based on a too simplistic repudiation of nationalism. We should admit the legitimacy of national feelings (and not be ashamed of them); we should not accept the misleading and false idea that something called Europe must be great, strong, united, prefabricated, and controlled from above to survive in the current economic, political, and military competition in the world. Europe is "a unity of diversities," and any attempt to unify it artificially would do more harm than good. Our first president, T. G. Masaryk, put the same idea very clearly in 1922. He said, "The task of Europe is to bring centralizing and autonomist forces into harmony. The unity and cohesion of Europe depend on this harmony." Europe is, in this interpretation, nothing more or less than a fragile balance of ethnic and cultural diversity. The challenge for Europe these days is, therefore, to give its integration the most proper direction and content to enhance that balance, not destroy it. My conclusion is simple: the search for integration is an endless process, and we all must have a chance to participate in it.

The Czech Republic would like to play an active part in the present European integration process as a reliable, stable, transparent, and self-confident partner. I can assure you that we do not want just to receive, that we are ready to give as well. We know that we have to solve our own problems and do not expect our European neighbors to solve them for us. I am very optimistic about our current success in approaching them, and I can assure you that we will not give up in our effort to get rid of the past and to become a free, democratic, efficient, and prosperous country in a free, democratic, efficient, and prosperous Europe.

19. Current Challenges and Conservative Solutions: The Czech Perspective

Introduction

I am very pleased to be here, to attend for the first time a conference of the British Conservative Party and to meet the leading representatives of conservative and other, ideologically similar, political parties from all over the world.

I have come here from a European country that, almost six years ago, started a radical systemic change. I have come here from a country that can now claim that communism is definitely over, that it is—for us—nearly a forgotten historic event, something rejected and refused by the vast majority of my countrymen, something remembered with nostalgia by only a very tiny minority of people in the country. Today, I dare to say that there are no more—and possibly fewer—"true believers" in communism or "fellow travelers" in my country than in Britain. It is like that because nothing persuades more than personal experience, and we were both punished and privileged to have had it.

Our country can be—despite all our doubts, questions, and self-criticism—proud of its favorable developments, of its political stability, of its social peace, of its macroeconomic indicators, of the fastest and most comprehensive privatization process, and of its rapid expansion of private initiative. And I should remind you of an inevitable step that was not sufficiently understood abroad when it was taken—the smooth, constitutionally founded division of the former Czechoslovakia into two independent and sovereign states. We achieved that without the slightest outburst of nationalism and without unfriendliness. That was a rare accomplishment.

The 1995 Conservative Party Conference Lecture, Blackpool, United Kingdom, October 11, 1995.

We have established both a free society, based on political pluralism, and a market economy, with private property, limited government, and drastic liberalization and deregulation. It is appropriate
to argue that we already have entered what we call the post-transformation stage. In that respect—measured by the structural parameters of the system, not by per capita gross domestic product—we
have become a "normal" European country.

I have come here also as a founder and chairman of a political
party with an ideology similar to yours. (We hesitated to give our
party the same name as yours when we founded it in the spring of
1991.) The formation of the Civic Democratic Party in our country
was the final blow to those who advocated the ideas of "unpolitical
politics," to those who saw the future as a world full of civic movements and temporary initiatives without party structures or clearly
defined organizational rules, to those who wanted a world based
on brave and innovative ideas implemented directly by enlightened
intellectuals who tried to stay above the complicated world of politics. Theirs was a dangerous dream of creating a new society that
would be better than the alternatives we knew.

Some of us knew that such a system would be structurally very
similar to the one we wanted to dismantle, and, for that reason, it was
important for us to establish a right-wing, pragmatic, conservative,
democratic, nonaristocratic, open, and nonexclusive political party.
We all know the results. We became the strongest party in the
country. We now lead a coalition government that has—ideologically—no counterpart in Central and Eastern Europe these days,
much to my regret.

Ideological Background

I would like to say a few words about the roots, the considerations,
and the ideas behind all that.

We started our Velvet Revolution, our systemic change, our fundamental transformation of the entire political, social, and economic
framework—not a reform, not perestroika—with a clear positive
vision of the society we wanted to live in. We had a vision of a free,
open society; we knew that after dismantling communist institutions
the resulting institutional vacuum had to be filled with an alternative
mechanism that would create social cohesion and make possible the
coordination of human activities. We learned from Hayek, Popper,

and other liberal and conservative thinkers that the evolution of human institutions, and especially the evolution of such complex systems as society, proceeds more by means of "human action" than of "human design"; that we must find the optimum balance between intentions and spontaneity, between the constructivism of political leaders and the unforeseeable behavior of millions of free citizens pursuing their dreams, hopes, and preferences; and that no sophisticated masterminding of such a process is possible or necessary.

All of that is, I believe, truly conservative. It is too early to judge the special Czech blend of vision and transformation strategy, but let me make some preliminary comments.

Our approach was undoubtedly influenced by the traditional Czech pragmatism and realism; by our strong democratic, nonaristocratic, almost plebeian traditions; by our evident lack of heroism; by our disbelief in authority, strong words, and formal gestures; and, finally, by uncertainty about our national identity, which had been lost, taken, or questioned so many times in the past.

Politically, our approach was based on something very close to British conservatism. We were directly influenced by you; we were inspired by the Thatcherite revolution in British politics two decades ago, by a political style based on a strong vision, on clear, transparent, and widely understandable ideas, on courage and persuasiveness; we were impressed by your success in achieving a dramatic resolution of an eternal human issue: placing the individual first and the state second. As the main slogan of our last elections, we accepted yours: "individual, family, municipality and state," in exactly that order.

In the field of economics and economic policy we were influenced more by American than European authors, by Milton Friedman, by the Chicago school, by James Buchanan and his public-choice school, by the criticisms of Keynesianism and, of course, by our own understanding of the irrationality, inefficiency, and inhumanity of a command economy. Because of that, we had no dreams about mixed systems, about third ways or different vintages of perestroika. That was our main reason for arguing strongly against popular (on the Continent) concepts like "social market economy," which in our country, and I guess in yours as well, is a term used by the opposition.

Finally, our approach to society and social mechanisms was influenced mostly by Hayek, by his ideas about government interventionism, about constructivism and social engineering, about the dangerous "pretense of knowledge," about the logic of an "evolutionary order," about the "fatal conceit." We learned a lot, and we do not intend to be deceived again.

I am deeply convinced that with such an approach we have found the best way to create a free, individually responsible, and moral society. We are sometimes accused of forgetting to mention adjectives other than "free." However, I believe that it is sufficient to guarantee freedom—individual happiness is up to each of us.

No End of History

The end of "hard" communism, both as an ideology and as a social system, gave birth to irresponsible, ahistoric, utopian dreams of or predictions about approaching the end of history and ideology. I have in mind the well-known book of Fukuyama and the subsequent debate. Such a stationary world cannot exist, and the debates in which we engage every day tell us that such a world will—we hope—never arrive. I feel that ideological controversies in our countries (and now I do not differentiate) demonstrate that we have to deal with the same debates as we did before. The eternal political fight is about the role of the individual in society, and the controversies about obligatory or voluntary memberships in professional chambers, about the role of collective bargaining, about the degree of social security, about regulation of financial markets—to name a few examples of recent hot topics in my country—or about agricultural policy, about the philosophy of the welfare state, about anti-dumping and protectionism, about the structure and mandates of European Union institutions—to cite examples from your country—reflect the same old dilemmas. In all of them, the issue is more or less individual freedom, more or less government control; in all of them the issue is how far we are ready to proceed on the slippery road to a Brave New World.

The discussion of European integration is a typical example. There is a tendency in Europe these days to pretend that this is not an ideological issue, that it is either a quasi-technical issue or simply self-evident, but that is not true. We are discussing "pure ideology"—big is supposed to be better than small, coordination from above to be better than the voluntary interplay of individual actors, protecting farmers to be better than protecting consumers, and so on. In a democratic society people have different and sometimes conflicting ideas, which should be discussed and not rejected a priori just because they do not reflect popular or fashionable opinion.

Let me say a few words about the process of European integration. The original concept of integration (elimination of barriers to the movement of people, ideas, goods and services, labor and capital) is something that most of us believe in, but that does not imply that we support ambitions to prefabricate all Europeans into a special breed of homo sapiens to be called *Homo europaeus*. I believe that the concept of integration—defined as the process of gradual elimination of all restrictions on the interplay of human beings—enjoys widespread support in Europe but that the idea of unification, which I interpret as integration plus the additional vision of the structure and organization of human society, is not so readily shared by all Europeans. It represents a different and more ambitious goal. I am a Euro-optimist regarding the future and the overall positive impact of European integration but a Eurorealist regarding our ability to unify Europe under a single ideological banner.

I do not believe that the process of European integration should be based on expectations that "European" feelings will be stronger than the national identities held by most Europeans—a shift of the fragile balance of "unity in diversity" toward more unity than diversity. Nor do I believe integration should be based on ambitions to create a strong, unified, and united entity able to compete with the United States and Japan or on temporary fashions in ideology, evident in current approaches to industrial and trade policy, social charter, environmental aspirations, and so on.

We all want a free Europe, we all want European institutions that would enhance the freedom of individuals living in Europe, we all want institutions that would make us happier and would make us all more prosperous. I do not want institutions that would try to force their own values, ambitions, or prejudices on us, institutions that would favor special interests at the cost of the interests of the whole.

Digression to Currency Union

The debate about a single European currency is a typical example. This institution, as any other, should be discussed using economic, not just political, arguments. Its eventual realization will bring about both costs and benefits, and it is necessary to recognize and compare them. The benefits are well known and undisputed. There will be efficiency gains connected with the completion of an integrated European market and with the elimination of transactions costs associated with separate national currencies.

The costs have rarely been discussed, and when they have been, the questions have not been answered. The costs will be unevenly distributed because of the heterogeneity of the European Union. This problem has been discussed in EU circles under the heading of cohesion. Will a single currency bring more or less cohesion? Will there be a widening or a narrowing of interregional differences? My argument is that attempting to fix currencies together—in advance of, and in the absence of, political and fiscal cohesion among the European states—is a very problematic issue. I do not think Europe is an optimal currency area. An optimal currency area exists where there is a high degree of factor mobility and stability in relative prices, where there is a high degree of openness inside the area and a much lower degree of openness between the area and the rest of the world, not to mention similar inflation rates, policy integration, and an efficient fiscal federalism based on the centralization of fiscal competences. I do not see that in Europe these days.

I am afraid Europe does not have enough relative wage flexibility, labor and capital mobility, and fiscal transfers to be able to guarantee an efficient adjustment mechanism for offsetting asymmetric regional shocks. The existence of a single currency deprives the states of a very important policy instrument for adjusting to internal or external supply or demand shocks, or both—the exchange rate. If there is no monetary instrument for adjustment, there can be a real (but asymmetric) adjustment only through the level of wages and unemployment or through migration. That situation will be very difficult to sustain politically. The example of German reunification is a warning when you see how big the fiscal transfers needed to overcome its consequences have been and will continue to be. I do not think such a degree of fiscal federalism is feasible in Europe, and, therefore, I do not consider a single currency an appropriate target for the foreseeable future.

Conclusion

Conservative parties have a permanent duty: to fight for their occasionally unpopular ideas, because that is the only way to keep them alive. I can assure you that this is exactly what we are doing. We have been significantly enriched by your example and by your long tradition, and we hope that our experience in dismantling communism and building a free society is of interest to you.

20. The Quality of Life, the Environment, and Systemic Change

The topic of your conference is very relevant to what is going on in this country, in this part of the world, and elsewhere; it is of great theoretical interest, and it is of practical interest as well.

I will not try to impose any official, authoritarian view upon you; I will only express my personal views that reflect my dual roles as an academic economist on the one hand and as a practical politician on the other. That special combination may be of some interest to the geographers, environmentalists, and other participants in your conference.

Let me start by stressing that my basic methodological assumption when thinking about the quality of life (without trying to define that term exactly) is that it is the logical outcome of the functioning of the system we live in. This systemic approach (and I would like to point out that I do not mean systematic or complex approach) is, in my opinion, absolutely crucial, because, according to that approach, the quality of life is the outcome of millions of decisions of millions of individuals; it is the result of their spontaneous behavior; it is not the result of anybody's policy, as is so often erroneously thought.

I am rather puzzled when I hear discussions about the environment that systematically overlook that crucial interrelationship. The role of an explicit policy is usually overstated; the role of rational, autonomous behavior of individual human beings in political, social, and economic spheres is underestimated or even forgotten. That is methodologically wrong as an explanation of reality, and it is extremely harmful as a guide for government policy. It is ideologically wrong because it reflects a disbelief in the rationality of the behavior of all of us and because it generates a false belief in the

Address delivered to the conference on "Quality of Life and Environment in Central Europe: Problems of Transition," Charles University, Prague, August 1994.

capacity of some of us to construct, to design better worlds for the rest of us. We used to live in such a world, and we do not want to do so again.

By dismantling communism and by creating a free society and a market economy we have, undoubtedly, made the most important contribution to improving the quality of life.

By introducing a rational economic system based on private property and an unregulated price mechanism, we created a valid economic, and therefore nature-saving, system, which has no alternative; we formed the elementary, systemic preconditions for our better future. Private property, rational prices, and individual responsibility are more important for environmental protection than are the activities of governments, of legislators, and of environmental organizations.

A free-market economic system, of course, is not sufficient. By introducing a free, democratic political system we created a mechanism for a rational process of public choice, of balanced decisionmaking at the macrolevel, that reflects the preferences and priorities of all members of society, not just of the political or professional elite.

I am very optimistic about our chances of solving the environmental problem because I am very optimistic about our achievements in overcoming our past and in transforming our countries. I am convinced that the Czech Republic has entered what we call the post-transformation stage and that other postcommunist countries will reach that stage soon. The new societal system is already here, but we should be aware of the fact that not all markets are fully efficient. That leads some of us to advocate more government intervention, but I hope past experience tells us clearly that a government failure is more dangerous and damaging than a market failure and that we should not advocate government intervention.

Maybe what I have been saying is self-evident to you and I am trying to open an already open door. I would be delighted if that were the case.

21. Konrad Adenauer and the Meaning of European Integration

To be awarded the Konrad Adenauer Prize is for me, and surely for any politician, a great honor, since it is named after a man who has meant, and still means, a great deal for this century. The stars of politicians generally fade rapidly, as time flows on after the end of their careers. There are a few politicians whose stars continue to shine for years, indeed, for decades after their demise, politicians who have left behind a legacy that cannot be ignored. Adenauer was unquestionably one of those, and that is why he can serve not only as a great example but also as a source of inspiration. He was not only chancellor of Germany but also chairman of the Christian Democratic Union in an extremely difficult, insecure, and troubled period, a period that in our current terminology would be called "an era of transformation." Those two positions remind me of a thing or two in my own life.

In the context that concerns us today, it must be stressed that Adenauer was not only a German politician, that (together with Ludwig Erhard) he was not only the initiator of the German postwar revival and of the economic miracle, but that he was also a great European. In the 1950s, as the world was emerging from the horrors of World War II, he emphasized and defended traditional European values and their universal validity, and he maintained that "the most fundamental duty of Europe is to be the homeland of freedom, culture, and progress" (1952). He feared that "in a world of superpowers, to insist on the idea of a nation-state is irresponsible and not in the interest of any nation" (1955), and that is why he regarded the "European integration process as the point of departure of German foreign political existence" (1955). What is equally important is that he considered "Europe" all the lands that had traditionally

Konrad Adenauer Foundation Prize acceptance speech, Prague, December 1993.

119

been thought of as European, not as just those countries that happened to be members of a particular postwar European entity, such as NATO. In 1967 he said in Madrid, "When we consider Europe, we must look to the East as well. These countries which have a rich European past are also part of Europe. These countries must have the possibility of entering Europe as well." That was Adenauer in 1967. I am afraid there are some people in Western Europe nowadays who seem to have forgotten that idea.

I would like to take this opportunity to state loud and clear that, even after four decades of life under a communist regime, we share his faith in European values, we share his conviction that European cooperation and European integration are imperative, and we share his insistence that Europe not be confined to its Western part alone. I am convinced that we must treat his legacy of ideas responsibly and carefully, but we must not regard it as dogma. It is our duty to distinguish the permanent aspects of that legacy from those that were determined by the specific conditions of the 1950s and by trends of thought that predominated at that time.

If I examine Adenauer's problems from that angle today, I have the impression that the original, too simplistic repudiation of nationalism needs to be reappraised—especially in light of our recent experience. We should admit the legitimacy of national feelings (and not be ashamed of them). At the same time it is essential to again compare the effects of mere coexistence and spontaneous cooperation among European states (often, but not always, nation-states) with those of the feasible alternative, which is not an intrinsic internationalism, combined with the natural identification of people with the continent on which they live, but rather reflects a somewhat artificial, bureaucratic supranationalism imposed from above.

I am sorry, but I find it difficult to identify with Adenauer's thought of 1960 that it is necessary to bring about a "close cohesion of the continent in order to be able to pursue correct policies." With a touch of exaggeration, I would say that that continental perception of the world was a direct reflection of the ideological paradigm of the first two-thirds of the 20th century. That period was characterized by a general loss of faith in the positive outcome of the unorganized coordination or cooperation of individual microsubjects—perfect competition in the economic sphere and coexistence of comparably great and comparably strong countries in the foreign policy sphere.

Instead, people became aware of the existence and economic strength of monopolies (that explains the origin of the theory of imperfect or monopoly competition of Joan Robinson and Edward Chamberlain), and they further recognized the existence and strength of the superpowers. That gave rise, in turn, to new political science hypotheses about the "balance of power" and about nuclear deterrence. Economists searched for a new balance in the model of imperfect competition, and political scientists looked for a balance among several superpowers (or various regional groupings) that would keep one another in check.

Thanks to that vision of the world, Europe bowed to the idea that it must be great, strong, and united in order to survive the economic, political, and military competition. It was feared that in all of those spheres Europe was lagging behind other powers or regions and that unless it united it would not stand a chance. Adenauer, too, frequently stressed the newly emerging "division of power in the world" and said that "the decline of European countries from the point of view of power is advancing at exceptional speed" (1967). At the same time, another perception, not of an economic but of a highly technocratic nature, was spreading. That perception was that technical progress required large dimensions, that is to say, big business, large firms, and powerful states or suprastate entities. Let us recall an almost symbolic European bestseller of the late 1960s, French journalist J. J. Servan Schreiber's *Le défi américain* (*The American Challenge*). I must insist that already at that time we in Prague were aware that Schreiber's was an erroneous perception of the world.

However, it was generally believed that there was no alternative. Either there would be an unregulated, uncoordinated, unorganized system (unfortunately, with bad results for some of the players because of their differing standards) or an interaction of some kind of "countervailing powers"—teams of approximately equally strong partners, which in certain instances would have to be created. There were many advocates of the idea of some sort of worldwide central management that would complement bureaucratic state intervention, which, thanks to the influence of Keynes, was advancing strongly at the national level.

In 1989 all of the barriers that had blocked our road to Europe during the previous decades collapsed—not, it is true, by the stroke of a magic wand, yet nevertheless at great speed and with relative ease. Four years later we realize that while some scope has been created for achieving all we regarded in the past as nothing more than a dream, there has been a simultaneous return to reality and a sobering up. And I am not referring merely to the sobering up of dreamers, who have been seeing the world through rose-colored spectacles, but even to that of practical-minded politicians.

At first glance it might have appeared that the rhetoric had not changed a great deal, but responsible politicians had begun to ask the right questions and soon became aware that the question of our present and future position in Europe was in fact the question of our national and state identity—of what we were able to offer others in a European context, of what we were able to request from them, of what we were capable of absorbing, and of what would make us advance further. So, these are not hypothetical but highly practical questions; they concern the formulation of our state and national interests.

The first three years of free Czechoslovakia were one phase of searching for this identity. After 40 years in a political vacuum, it became evident that the search was far from easy. That difficult and painful quest finally reached a point where the existing Czecho-Slovak state arrangement ceased to meet the needs of Slovak national emancipation. The partition of the common Czechoslovak state must, therefore, be seen as a peaceful agreement on matters that elsewhere threaten to become, and in some places have become, grave national conflicts and as an agreement enabling the Slovaks and the Czechs to begin creating their own reliable foundations for their own domestic and foreign policies. Everything that, had the common state been preserved, might have turned into insoluble conflicts has now lost its dangerous explosive charge and, instead, has turned into subtle distinctions and diversities that are understandable and normal in relations between independent states.

I would like to stress that the advanced West European states, which in the past decades participated in the process of European integration, entered that process as nonproblematic, stable political and economic actors. Their political (democratic) and economic (free market) compatibility was basically secure. Adherence to European culture and to European civilization was in no way questioned in the case of those states that in the past had deviated in one way or another from democratic political standards for a time (Greece, Spain, Portugal). But what is most important is that all those countries approached integration with no problems about their identity, something we must regard as the fundamental prerequisite of a position of equality within a higher entity. That is probably why there was no danger that the unity of integration would eclipse everything that makes Europe what it is, namely, "a unity of diversities," as our first president, T. G. Masaryk, stressed some 70 years ago.

The position of the Central and East European countries that have liberated themselves, and in some cases are still liberating themselves, from communist domination differs from that of their Western partners, since they are all young states that emerged after the collapse of three essentially supranational empires (the Austrian, the Ottoman, and the Russian), which in the past were a barrier to the political ambitions of the nations they embraced. The fragile and in some ways flawed security and political system of Central and Southeast Europe in the 1920s and 1930s collapsed under the pressure of Nazi aggression. There appeared different perceptions of the world with regard to the threat of monopolies and the character of technical progress: the effect of Keynesian-style state interventionism, political engineering in the setup of the world, the imbalance in the dynamics of individual states and regions, the economic growth factor, and so forth.

That has been reflected in an entirely different social science paradigm: not big, but small, is beautiful; there is an emphasis on openness—that is to say, on an integral, worldwide framework of economic processes; trade and technical progress are likewise stressed; and there is a belief in the market and not in the state. I am fully convinced that all this—after a normal passage of time between the idea and its practical application—will enter the universal awareness of the public and politicians and, ultimately, will take shape as practical policies. As Ortega y Gasset clearly pointed out, "The ideas of intellectuals require a long time before they become an historical force, since in order to do this they must cease to be mere ideas but change into commonplace truths, into habit and public opinion."

For all those reasons, we regard the entire European integration process as the indisputable, natural starting point of Czech foreign policy, and it must always be accorded the importance it deserves. I think integration is precisely what Europe has been trying to achieve for centuries, at times peacefully and at times with excessive violence. Europe has been striving toward that objective with ever-greater vigor and determination since the beginnings of the European Community, which was established with the best of knowledge and intentions in the 1950s. That was also the goal for which Adenauer worked with all his energy.

A reappraisal of no smaller dimensions is now confronting Europe after the collapse of communism, after the fall of the Iron Curtain. This process of reappraisal must be founded on the ability to stand aside from everyday reality, from the details of the present, and take a wider historical view.

Since I am looking to the past for support, I cannot fail to quote the prophetic words Masaryk pronounced as far back as 1922: "The task of Europe is to bring centralizing and autonomist forces into harmony. The unity and cohesion of Europe depend on this harmony. But unity does not mean uniformity. Europe is made up of an ethnological and cultural diversity. Europe has advanced towards diversity over millennia, and that is why its cohesion must be organized in accordance with a historical principle and, at the same time, with existing natural, national and other diversities." Ortega y Gasset used similar terms when he said in West Berlin in 1949 that "Europe is not an object but a balance. . . . The balance or disposition of forces is a reality which essentially rests on the existence of plurality. If plurality is lost, dynamic unity wastes away." He used that criterion to distinguish "European" centuries from centuries of "particularism." If we are to use the same formulation, I think we must carefully observe the phase in which we happen to be at this very moment.

I would like to take advantage of the fact that we are in Prague to formulate a few thoughts from a purely Czech point of view, in other words, from the point of view of a small Central European postcommunist, and today already free and democratic, country. I cannot fail to mention that during the past 40 years Europe (I am referring to democratic Western Europe) was something that the Czechs regarded as an almost ideal community of which they longed to become part. Yet it was clear to us that there was absolutely no scope for political moves toward that goal. That led to the oversimplification of our thinking—as is the case in all such instances in the lives of individuals and state entities—to an unrealistic picture both of ourselves and of Europe.

It might have been possible to allow the state ambitions of the postcommunist nations to take root and for them to solve their concealed or open conflicts, internal or external, by normal political means. Instead, many acts of violence were committed during and after World War II that only put those conflicts into cold storage. Subsequently, the icy blanket of communist dictatorship covered everything for 40 years. The postcommunist countries, therefore, face a double task today: finding their own identities and not losing them straightaway on their road to Europe. This is probably much more difficult than, say, an observer in Brussels might think at first glance. The Czech Republic, too, is confronted with this dual and difficult task. We naturally want to become part of advanced Europe, and I am convinced that we possess the fundamental prerequisites for doing so, perhaps even more so than some other countries. But we wish to become part of it as a sovereign political entity, as the Czech Republic, which will be neither lost nor dissolved in Europe, and which has something to offer to the entity it will join.

Hence, we Europeans face a double challenge. The Czech Republic faces the challenge of rapidly creating the internal conditions for our political and economic integration into Europe (and I repeat that I believe that we have made significant headway on this road). And advanced Europe faces the challenge of giving integration the most proper direction and content. We cannot expect Europe to wait until we solve our own problems, and I would like to add straightaway that we are not asking for that. Instead, we ask for a realistic timetable for the major moves toward integration and, above all, for a permanent, pragmatic scrutiny of the nature of this integration. I would like to express my most profound conviction that countries such as the Czech Republic are capable of contributing a thing or two to the European entity, and that it is therefore worthwhile to reconsider and give the finishing touches to the procedure, scope, and technique of integration processes in discussion with those who are to be involved. The communist past has made us quite sensitive to certain matters, which—since in Western Europe they never reached the extremes they did in Eastern Europe—can easily be underestimated. It is our duty to point out those dangers and not permit them to spread to the whole of Europe, albeit under different slogans. We would genuinely like to play an active part in all this.

PART IV

THE CZECH REPUBLIC IN THE WORLD

22. Partnership for Peace Speech

The signing of the Partnership for Peace framework document provides an excellent opportunity for the first visit of the prime minister of the Czech Republic to the seat of NATO and for an explanation of the basic approaches to safeguarding our external security.

As you know, after 40 years under a communist regime, the Czech Republic has become again an independent and sovereign state devoted to the principles of democracy, freedom, and the rule of law. Because of that, our concept of security is based, not only on the values of sovereignty, freedom, and democracy, but also on the resolution of our citizens to defend them.

I can assure you that the security of our country as well as our contribution to European peace and stability represent a top priority for the Czech government. In this context, we are well aware of the fact that the basic preconditions for the security of the Czech Republic are internal political and economic stability on the one hand and the ability and willingness to protect our security by our own means on the other. However, the security of the Czech Republic—as one of the smaller states in the center of Europe—also depends in a very important sense on external conditions and international guarantees.

The very positive relations between the Czech Republic and the alliance are well known. Our current pro-Atlantic orientation is not short-sighted and does not arise from a direct or imminent external threat; it is, rather, the natural expression of a political and cultural identity and of the values on which our society is based. For us, NATO is an alliance of countries that share the same values we do, countries united by their will to defend those values. NATO has proved its viability even since the threat that led to its creation faded away with the breakdown of communism.

Speech delivered at the signing of the Partnership for Peace framework document, Brussels, March 1994.

We consider the alliance the most reliable way of safeguarding our security, and I would like to stress here that future NATO membership is our undisputed strategic aim. But, given current circumstances, we perceive the integration of the Czech Republic into NATO as a gradual process. Its success and rapidity depend on the efforts of all the parties concerned.

Since the termination of the Cold War, we have been, and the alliance itself has been, facing new challenges. It is necessary to seek a new balance in the transatlantic relation, to formulate new strategic concepts, to define the delicate relationship between existing members and new applicants for membership. It is necessary to preserve NATO strong and functional according to the letter of the original Washington treaty.

From the Czech point of view, the January summit of NATO was an appropriate reaction to those challenges. We attach great importance to the confirmation of the openness of the alliance, and we consider the initiative that has led to the Partnership for Peace a step in the right direction even if the partnership is undoubtedly the result of a compromise between the various interests of NATO members and their partners.

What we especially appreciate about the Partnership for Peace is that

- it increases U.S. interest and participation in European security arrangements, which is, for us, a precondition for the future stability of the whole Continent;
- it provides space for practical rapprochement between the Czech Republic and NATO and offers the prospect of our future membership in the alliance;
- it stipulates consultations between NATO and its partners in the case of a threat to their territorial integrity, sovereignty, or security; and
- each agreement between NATO and a partner is individualized according to each partner's own needs and means.

The Czech government accedes to the Partnership for Peace and shall define its own conceptions of the contents of its partnership agreement in the near future. Together with 16 NATO member-states, we intend to prepare it as the foundation of our individual program of partnership between the Czech Republic and the alliance.

If we are to use the Partnership for Peace as a step toward future alliance membership, it is, in our opinion, important to preserve the balance between the political and military parts of the partnership and between our own and NATO's obligations—between costs and benefits for all sides. Under the Partnership for Peace, the Czech Republic intends to prepare itself to be able to participate in all aspects of the alliance—including reaching compatibility and inter-operability of armed forces, sharing of expenses, and completion of domestic legislation necessary for the participation of the Czech Republic in joint exercises as well as in possible future missions. At this moment, I would like to tell you that the Czech government yesterday decided to increase our participation in peacekeeping forces in Bosnia.

The partnership will have—besides its political and military value—its costs. The Czech Republic is ready to bear its share of those costs, although it is difficult to estimate their level now. Neither the Partnership for Peace nor future NATO membership will be for us a "free ride."

At the same time, we expect that the alliance will approach the issue of strengthening the partnership with the Czech Republic with utmost responsibility in the political as well as in the military field, taking into account the implicit and spontaneous unity of the community of democratic countries, the solidarity of its individual members, and the indivisibility of their security.

The signature of the Czech Republic, attached to the Partnership for Peace framework document, is a logical, justified, and desirable step that confirms not only our expectations but also our will and preparedness to take part in the protection of common interests and the security of the transatlantic area.

23. The Common Crisis: Is There Any?

Being known as a person who always accepts other people's suggestions, a few months ago I accepted the suggested title of my speech, "The Common Crisis." But several days ago when I started to seriously think about what to say, I modified the title slightly, adding the question, "Is There Any?" The reason for the addition is that I am the last one who would call our situation—either at home or in Europe or in the whole world—a crisis. Such a pessimistic label seems to me inappropriate. For me the term "crisis" connotes a situation where everything goes down, not up; where there are questions without answers; where there are problems without solutions; where there is a lack of elementary social cohesion and mutual understanding; where there is no dynamic, just a stationary state. That is not what I see when I look around.

I prefer to start my discussion today with different assumptions. We live in a real, not a hypothetical, world, in a world with real—which means imperfect—people, with imperfect social institutions, with many issues that remain to be resolved. But in that world we see tangible results, visible improvements, and innovative solutions to many difficult problems.

The postcommunist and post–Cold War era has witnessed visible movement forward. To interpret it differently means to be disappointed with what has happened since 1989. For me, we are moving toward, we are on the road to, a better world, a world without totalitarian regimes (at least in Europe and America, our common Atlantic region), without threatening military structures, without totally inefficient economic systems, without overly ideological thinking. We have not yet entered heaven and we will never make it, but I am confident that we are on the right track. I know there are people among us who see crisis in any moment when there is

---

Notes for a speech delivered at the New Atlantic Initiative Conference, Prague, May 11, 1996.

no central authority in full control of all events; when there is no dirigisme from above; when we witness more spontaneity in human behavior than somebody planned; whenever there is anything new, unknown, unplanned, and unprepared; when the old clichés are lost or forgotten. I do not belong to that group.

We have undoubtedly entered a new period, but I see it as a chance, not as a problem.

I know, of course, that human society is very fragile (and vulnerable to all kinds of disturbances), and to think that we will be able to move forward without a permanent effort, without daily involvement of all of us in a never-ending fight for freedom, would be a fatal mistake, a "fatal conceit," and would take us on "the road to serfdom," which some of us know too well. To think that the collapse of communism and its probable definitive end are a final victory, the "end of history," would be very costly. We all see around us new dangers, new blind alleys, new attempts to create Brave New Worlds based on very promising rhetoric, on more or less sincere intentions but on wrong ambitions and false assumptions about human behavior.

Even though I expressed my strong disagreement with the term "crisis" in the title of this session, I accept the adjective "common." With all of its historical and cultural differences, human society is more homogeneous than some of us assume. I agree with those who say that there are common answers to our problems. In addition to that, I believe that the answers are simple, more or less known and old-fashioned, and realizable. I am optimistic and I agree with one of the heroes of the Atlantic movement, Ronald Reagan, who many years ago said, "The experts tell us there are no simple answers to our difficulties. They are wrong. There are simple answers, just not easy ones." It is our task to look for and find them. I hope this conference will help us do that.

The ambition of our conference is, of course, not so general. We are interested in a closer issue, in transatlantic relations. The idea of transatlantic cooperation between Europe and North America we are talking about was born at the end of World War II. The tragic experience of our fathers and grandfathers with fascist dictatorships, with communism, and with the devastating war and their resolution not to go through those things again led to many postwar activities and to the formation of several international organizations, especially NATO.

Transatlantic cooperation was for decades kept together by an imminent communist threat, and we, subconsciously, accepted the idea that NATO is an anti-communist bloc and nothing else. With the end of communism the common enemy disappeared, and some of us seem to be at a loss about what to fight for.

I am not. For me, the transatlantic community was never connected solely with one past enemy. It has deeper roots and a stronger basis. It is based *on ideas, not on enemies*. It is connected with the tradition of freedom, democracy, and market economy. European and American liberalism (in its original, European meaning) represents our common cultural heritage, which we try to keep alive for future generations on both sides of the Atlantic ocean. We are committed to that duty, and we have to be vigilant in all spheres, including the security one.

I am aware of the existing dangers and know that, for the time being, they are more in the field of ideas than in the field of security. Some of them are "domestic" and are connected with new attempts to corporatize and syndicalize our societies, with attempts to legislatively support organizations and associations—thus dividing us and filling the space between the individual and the state at the expense of both and denying the elementary principles of a liberal society. Such approaches are justified, erroneously, by well-intended people who advocate, not further reductions of statism through liberalization, deregulation, and privatization (not just in the economic sphere), but new versions of collectivism; not overall healthy competition, but more and more ideas controlled by experts, professionals, and "better" people; not the acceptance of incrementalism and improvements of Pareto optimality, but isolated, absolutist "solutions" to particular problems; not a coherent society but new "feudalities" (to use Ludwig Erhard's term).

Such tendencies, when prevailing at home, will have enormous influence on international relations, on the whole of transatlantic cooperation, and we should not underestimate them. Our foreign policy reactions and initiatives are less autonomous than is often assumed, and their roots in domestic ideological tenets are very deep.

I see the danger of the increase of *isolationist* tendencies in both Europe and America, even if the increase is for different reasons. In Europe it is because of more deepening than widening of an integration philosophy, because of less vigorous market forces and less vigorous individualist traditions. In America it is because of the prevalence of new, less liberal ideologies and because of traditional self-centeredness in world affairs. I see external dangers as well, but I consider them less threatening than our own deficiencies.

At the beginning of my speech I rejected the assumption of the existence of a common crisis. I can, however, imagine the arrival of such a crisis at the moment we close ourselves off from, instead of opening ourselves to, both ideas and trade. For several decades we in this country lived in a closed society, and we know what that means. We know that it means stressing differences and hatred instead of searching for commonalities and friendship. I believe the original postwar transatlantic idea arose as a reaction to our prewar closedness, and we should not repeat our mistakes. The disappearance of one common enemy should not demotivate us. We know that the slippery road to serfdom is not very far away and that some parts of the road may offer seductive views of natural beauty.

24. The Roles of Domestic and External Factors in the Integration of Former Communist Lands into the World Economy

Introduction

Even if it is impossible to add anything unknown or extraordinarily important to the growing literature in this field, let me make several comments from my special perspective. Regardless of the first positive and doubtless promising results and achievements of economic transformation, former communist countries still have tremendous problems to solve and a long way to go. Nobody knows it, or perhaps should know it, better than this distinguished audience. The members of the Mont Pèlerin Society have been for four and a half decades trying to warn all of us—and especially one group, the irresponsible intellectuals—of the dangers of communism, statism, and collectivism and to turn our attention to the vulnerability of democratic institutions, of the market economy, and, therefore, of the whole free world.

My starting point is that democracy, freedom, and a market economy cannot be transplanted to an unprepared soil by decree, by lecturing, or by giving well-intentioned and good advice. It is not sufficient to translate one or another of the best or most democratic constitutions and to introduce it by command from above; it is not sufficient to send groups of advisers, to write off some debts, or to grant modest financial injections. The establishment of a free and democratic society and of a functioning market economy cannot be achieved by a single act based on human design. Our conservative philosophy tells us that transformation is a prolonged process of human action with millions of actors playing their own roles; that

Address delivered to the annual meeting of the Mont Pèlerin Society, Vancouver, September 1992.

it is a multidimensional process (because society cannot be compartmentalized); a process of time-consuming evolution of thousands of institutions and of the modes of human conduct that accompany them; a process of mutually reinforcing or mutually weakening attempts, efforts, and achievements of individual men and women with their own interests, dreams, prejudices, and capabilities.

The systemic transformation of a communist country, therefore, takes time. If the transforming country has a clear, strong, and convincing vision of where it wants to go, a pragmatic, flexible, and understandable reform strategy (how to get there), a sufficient degree of political and social cohesion, and bold and inspiring politicians, the results do come and the transformation can be successful. If such preconditions do not exist—and in most former communist countries they do not—there is no way of avoiding the reform trap and a vicious circle of small, partial, and overcautious reform measures (with mostly negative consequences) and total disintegration of the economy and of the whole society.

The task of responsible politicians is to keep moving ahead, not to stop, not to create wrong expectations; to secure visible, demonstrable achievements, because half measures, hesitation, lack of courage and capacity to guide, to govern, or to make decisions mean opening the doors to failure.

The Role of External Factors

Before starting a more detailed discussion of decisive domestic factors, I will make a few comments about the external side of the whole transformation process. My experience tells me that reform begins and ends at home and that the role of external factors is relatively small—definitely smaller than is usually thought. The stress on external factors turns our attention to wrong arguments and encourages the widespread belief that outside forces control the transformation process, which is wrong and, in addition, politically dangerous. I hesitate to discuss the role of external factors here, where everybody knows the work of Peter Bauer and his almost canonical arguments about the pitfalls of external aid in the development process, but the whole discussion has an impact that should not be underestimated.[1]

---

[1] See Peter Bauer, "Western Subsidies and Eastern Reform," *Cato Journal* 11, no. 3 (Winter 1992): 343–53.

There is no doubt that there are some very important positive external factors:

- the rapidly growing flow of visitors and businesspeople from abroad, who bring with them market-oriented attitudes, habits, and experience;
- the growing international trade in goods and services, which destroys the long-prevailing logic of semiautarchic centrally planned economies and of highly sheltered markets, undermines the economic and political power of domestic monopolies, and brings into the transforming country real competition and world standards;
- foreign real investments in a situation where property rights are already clearly defined and reasonably protected;
- macroeconomic stand-by arrangements (stabilization funds), which are absolutely necessary for moments of price deregulation, of foreign trade liberalization, and of convertibility introduction in countries with zero hard currency reserves and high hard currency debts.

There are marginal external factors that are considered positive by many people but that may have, in practice, effects that turn out to be negative. In this group belong

- technical assistance and consulting, which are offered either by extremely expensive private firms with insufficient understanding of the transformation problems and of the countries in question or by foreign governments or international institutions that very often employ people with a dirigiste or openly socialist outlook who are practically opposed to the transformation task;
- financial assistance coming from international lending institutions that have a deeply rooted tendency to favor government projects, not the creation of a strong private sector.

We have to face, however, additional external factors with fully negative consequences for the transformation process:

- long-standing or newly created trade barriers in individual countries or in regional blocs (recent restrictions on Czechoslovak steel exports to European Community countries or cement exports to Austria, for example);

- new international (mostly regional) organizations with an almost forced participation and a constructivist philosophy, which try to intervene and which absorb an extremely scarce resource—experienced staff in public service and the academy;
- promises of debt reduction or of debt cancellation, which suggest strange rules of the game—including the possibility of not meeting one's obligations;
- statist or collectivist ideologies and procedures imported from abroad that are not totally damaging in fully developed market economies but are harmful in newly born democracies and fragile markets.

On the whole, the contribution of external factors is, in my opinion, at best very limited. The West should, therefore, not regard them as of vital importance for the transformation process. The only way to create the conditions necessary for economic advance and growth in the postcommunist world is to move toward a market economy and private property as fast as possible.

Domestic Factors

My active involvement in the transformation process as well as my theoretical understanding of its subtleties, peculiarities, and pitfalls; my country's experience; and my interpretation of events in other postcommunist countries suggest some factors that contribute to the apparent lack of success of transformation processes all over the world.

Many countries (or, more accurately, reform politicians in many countries) start the whole process with faulty visions. Analyzing explicit or implicit visions, one is permanently confronted with nonnegligible residual effects of socialist (or collectivist or interventionist) doctrines, dogmas, and ideas on the minds of both politicians and common citizens in transforming countries. Those deeply rooted misconceptions and prejudices are usually hidden behind the facade of words like "reform," "liberalization," and "privatization" and can be revealed only by more careful study. The third-way thinking still represents—with the exception of one or two countries—a real danger that should not be underestimated.

The visions of the post-transformation world are supplemented by a strong belief in the necessity of constructivism and government masterminding during the transformation process itself. The basic

Hayekian dilemma of human design versus human action is intellectually more and more understood, but everybody (especially the opposition) wants perfect, detailed reform blueprints (as regards substance and timing) and a perfect cost/benefit analysis of systemic transformation. Such blueprints and calculations are not possible and not necessary. But our unwillingness and inability to produce them are a source of permanent criticism. The reform strategy must be flexible, and deregulation, liberalization, and privatization must be realized at a very early stage of reform.

Some reform measures can be taken overnight, but others take time. The evolution of political and economic institutions—political parties, private firms, banks, and financial intermediaries—is much slower than the collapse of central planning, and the initial results of the political and economic changes are far from optimal. Political life and parliamentary pluralism need strong political parties and an oligopolistic (but not monopolistic) political "market," but postcommunist countries have many and, therefore, weak political groupings (it is difficult to call them parties), and the atomistic structure of that market makes it difficult to put together the necessary political consensus. In the economy it is otherwise. We would need "perfect" competition with many participating economic agents, but we have inherited administratively formed monopolies and oligopolies. Both markets are weak and, therefore, less efficient than expected.

Expectations are not immediately fulfilled. Relatively inefficient political and economic processes (in the first stages of reform) and an aggressive social demagogy organized by left-wing political parties create a feeling of lack of success and undermine support for continuation of the reform process. Without a patient explanatory crusade on the part of reform politicians, public support is lost—as has happened in some countries already—and democratic elections bring to the fore less reform-minded politicians.

The sudden opening of freedom together with a sort of ideological vacuum create the opportunity for pursuing false ideas, values, and priorities. The most dangerous are, undoubtedly, the nationalistic ambitions of some political leaders (and of their followers), which push aside basic liberal values and turn popular attention from crucial political and economic reform measures. Precious time is lost, human patience is exhausted, the room for maneuvering is significantly restricted. In my own country separatist tendencies are gaining momentum, and economic reform (and its alleged errors) is not the most controversial issue of the day. National emancipation—as we discovered—is difficult to realize in a former federation, and the splitting of countries is unavoidable, whether we like it or not.

25. Foreign Aid for a Postcommunist Country

After three years of a relatively successful fundamental systemic transformation of the Czech economy and society, my experience tells me that the role of external factors in the process is relatively small and that reform begins and ends at home. Transforming a postcommunist country into a functioning market economy and into a free society requires, first, a clear vision of the goal the reformers pursue; second, a clear and pragmatic strategy to achieve it; and third, the ability of politicians to mobilize sufficient political support for the implementation of the transformation program. Those domestic preconditions are crucial for the success of the changes and cannot be supplemented by any form of foreign aid or assistance.

That fact is not always understood in the West, and extensive Western aid programs, or a lack thereof, are often seen as a cardinal condition for either the success or the failure of reforms.

We do not believe that debt relief or write-offs can really do more than undermine the credibility of the country, with all the negative consequences that entails. We do not think that a new Marshall Plan could save the postcommunist countries if they are not be able to help themselves first.

What we really need—instead of aid—is exchange. By exchange I mean symmetrical relations based on the principle of equivalence. We do not need one-way transfers because they tend to be misused, misdirected, or misplaced. They are usually not taken seriously by either side. I have in mind financial aid, gifts, technical assistance, and consulting. However, we do need exchange of people, ideas, and goods organized in such a way that both sides of the deal benefit. This argument may seem to be too abstract, but I am convinced it deserves to be developed and converted into working instructions for those who are engaged in the transformation endeavor.

Speech delivered to the Bretton Woods Committee, Washington, D.C., October 1993.

I would like to stress the importance of the macroeconomic stand-by arrangements of the International Monetary Fund and the structural adjustment loans of the World Bank in the early liberalization phase of reform. Those stabilization funds proved to be absolutely necessary at the time of price deregulation, foreign trade liberalization, and convertibility introduction. The precondition for their positive impact on the economy is, however, a strong reform package (including restrictive macropolicies) and the government's determination to implement it. We were fortunate that our reform program did not need to be designed by foreign experts, that our consistent and radical package was prepared by ourselves and fully supported by the citizens of the country, and that the endorsement of it by the IMF was mainly a positive signal for the outside world.

Our experience proves that, provided the right financial and exchange rate policies are in place, the need for external stabilization funds is very short-lived. However, we are still taking advantage of having a financial program with the IMF even if we do not need to draw upon its resources. We consider the program's positive-signal effect on the financial world very important.

How do we see the assistance of international financial institutions in our contemporary situation when the basic framework of a market economy is already in place? Here I would like to join the ongoing discussions about the role of the European Bank for Reconstruction and Development in Central and Eastern Europe.

We need international financial institutions to take the risk. By taking the risk, I mean their concentration on taking an active role in financing our newly born private sector on normal commercial principles, using their vast risk assessment abilities, financial strength, and access to international capital markets. We do not need them when they concentrate predominantly on catalyzing loans for big multinationals that intend to invest in our country. Those companies can easily do so by themselves if the project in question is worth undertaking. We do not need international financial institutions to prefer large infrastructural projects with government participation only. We do not need them to operate with only government guarantees for their loans. The government in our situation is overburdened by requests for its guarantees for all kinds of projects, and everybody knows that this condition is counterproductive both for financial stability and for effective allocation of resources in general.

We need international financial institutions to fill in certain gaps in our financial markets caused by a still weak and vulnerable banking sector that is hardly able to finance large projects on long-term conditions. We need them to proliferate financial know-how that is still insufficient in postcommunist economies.

We would welcome their support of our export promotion programs that are an extremely important tool for reorientation of our exports to new solvent markets (after the collapse of the traditional ones in the East). We would also welcome their support of our efforts to give momentum to our newly established capital market.

I am sure there are many other fields where Western assistance could be beneficial for both the providers and the recipients. But the crucial thing the West could do for the success of the unprecedented transformation process in postcommunist countries is to open markets for our exports. The main danger for us is attempts to introduce protectionist measures against our exports; it is the unwillingness of some governments to approve necessary steps for liberalization of international trade; it is the increasing influence of pressure groups and lobbies that would sacrifice the prosperity of the world to their partisan interests.

We appreciate very much that the Bretton Woods institutions have recently voiced their influential disapproval of those dangerous tendencies. We fully share the view that the prosperity of the world can be achieved only through further liberalization of international trade.

We are convinced that only a standard market economy based on sound financial grounds and operating in a liberal economic environment can achieve a stable level of prosperity. Only under those conditions could foreign aid and assistance have positive marginal returns.

26. Margaret Thatcher and the Czech Republic

It is really a great privilege for me to receive an honorary degree from your university. I take it as a personal honor, the first one awarded me in your country, and, at the same time, I take it as an honor for my country. I know that I have received it—and now I quote from the remarks I heard here several minutes ago—for my achievements as finance minister and prime minister of the Czech Republic and, in particular, for the transformation of the Czech economy through my liberalization policies.

I am especially honored to receive this degree from the hands of your chancellor, Lady Thatcher, whose explicit and implicit role in our Velvet Revolution and in the following radical restructuring of our whole society has been enormous and still has not been fully appreciated and recognized either here or in our part of the world. There were, of course, urgent and serious domestic reasons for dismantling communism and for attempting to create a free society, but the revolution in Central and Eastern Europe, in some respects, actually started in Great Britain at the moment of the victory of the Conservative Party in the elections of 1979 and at the moment of the appointment of Margaret Thatcher as prime minister.

Margaret Thatcher triggered—not just in the political, economic, and social fields but also in the sphere of ideology and in the more general moral and cultural dimensions of human life—a process the outcome of which probably exceeded her original aims and ambitions. She attacked *the expanding state*—which was and still is a dominant tendency of the 20th century, of the century of socialisms with a variety of confusing adjectives—and was *the first to do so with visible success.* She demonstrated that it was possible to break the

---

Address delivered on the occasion of being awarded an honorary doctor of sciences degree by the University of Buckingham, United Kingdom, February 24, 1996.

statist tendency, which was considered by the majority of intellectuals and social scientists of this century (from Schumpeter to Galbraith) to be almost an iron law of history. She demonstrated that it was possible to return to the liberal social order.

In Great Britain you had to deal with a softer version of a regulated and interventionist society, but I know that did not make it easier to convince people to cooperate, because the failure of the system was less visible, less transparent, less dramatic. In our case, the errors, failures, and tragedies of a much harder socialism were easier to see, to understand, to refute. But your political and especially economic and social reforms were for us—in Central and Eastern Europe and especially in my own country—an inspiration and a model. We understood that we had to start with a strong vision of where to go, be able to formulate and realize a feasible strategy for getting there, and win popular support for our efforts.

When I look back now, at more than six years of radical transformation of our whole society, I see that we had to face *similar challenges*. We had to maintain our vision of freedom and liberty against all forms of leftist arguments; we had to survive populist attacks concentrating on the short-term costs of our radical treatment of society and the economy; we had to convince people that we were not selling spiritual values for material ones; and we had to defend the benefits of spontaneous "human action" against the constructivism and dirigisme of "human design," to use Hayek's terminology.

My defense of the idea of market economy has not been based on economic arguments only, because a market economy is not merely a mechanism to ensure higher living standards and economic rationality. It is also the basis for the formation of a new moral system, which had to replace the false morality of the socialist society and its distorted relationship between the individual and society. Because of that, our Velvet Revolution was not only a transformation of economic institutions but also a profound change in the thinking and behavioral patterns of the whole society.

We have learned that the fundamental transformation of the whole societal structure is a very delicate *mixture* of political, social, economic, and spiritual events and that any one aspect of that mixture reinforces others. We have understood that it is impossible to go ahead in just one area because doing so would create a situation similar to an immunity reaction to an alien tissue in a human body.

Thanks to our comprehension of that fact, we proceed simultaneously in all directions.

The transformation of Czech society was based on three catchwords: liberalization, deregulation, and privatization.

We have proved that the liberalization and deregulation of markets and the resulting diminution of government intervention are necessary for changing the whole system, but we also realized that that was not sufficient. Those transformation measures plus waiting for an evolutionary emergence of efficient markets would take too long and would be too costly. Therefore, they had to be supplemented with radical privatization. We managed to effect the quickest and most extensive transfer of property rights (at least from government to private individuals). Now, five years after its beginning, the massive privatization is practically over. We therefore dare say that the country has entered what we call the post-transformation stage.

The communist regime in our country is already history, but the fact that we lived through it gives us, surprisingly, something positive. It makes us extremely sensitive to all kinds of deficiencies, disturbances, and violations of human freedom, which occur even in countries where democratic traditions have prevailed for decades or centuries. And this is a very productive asset. It makes us strong opponents of all the forms of soft socialism we see around us.

27. The University of Chicago and I

In the recent past my name has often been mentioned together with that of the University of Chicago—partly incorrectly, partly correctly. I have never had a chance to study here, but the well-known London journal *The Economist* several days after my appointment as minister of finance at the end of 1989 informed its readers that I had studied at the University of Chicago. Since then, that mistake has been quoted hundreds of times, and there is no way to correct it.

There have been spiritual links, however. I spent years studying the works of Milton Friedman, George Stigler, Gary Becker, and others (starting in the second half of the 1960s). In August 1989—coming here at the invitation of Jack Gould (then dean of the Graduate School of Business)—I had my first chance to see the campus, the buildings, several members of the faculty, and even to give a short luncheon talk. Today is my second chance—but in a totally different capacity.

At home and elsewhere in Europe I am called a "monetarist," or an exponent of Chicago views. For me it is an honor; it is meant, however, as an offense. I would like to stress that I do not deny the inspiration—for my life as well as my work—that I got from your university.

University of Chicago scholars helped me to understand economics better, to understand its methodology, the role of the market in society, the role of the state in a free-market economy, the role of money, and so on. There were other authors who influenced me, but they were not concentrated in a single university and did not have such a coherent approach. In the second half of the 1960s, while writing my doctoral dissertation on inflation, I discovered Milton Friedman, his *Restatement of the Quantity Theory of Money* and his *Essays in Positive Economics*, and I became a true believer. Friedman

---

Notes for a speech delivered at the University of Chicago, May 1, 1995.

was important to me methodologically (positive vs. normative economics; instrumentalism of scientific assumptions, *de gustibus non est disputandum*; generality, sometimes called imperialism of economic science; the economics of information); he was important to me from the point of view of ideas about economic policy (fixed vs. flexible rules, monetarism vs. Keynesianism); he was important to me ideologically *(Capitalism and Freedom, Free to Choose)*; and, finally, he was important to me from the point of view of a broader approach to life.

All that helped me (and us) to understand the tenets of the old communist regime and its oppressive character and irrationality. With that Chicago background, I have had no dreams about so-called third ways, about perestroika, about the reformability of communism.

At the same time, the works of other economists, sociologists, and lawyers from Chicago (not the works of specialized sovietologists) helped us to understand the logic of communist economy and society.

With Milton Friedman I have always interpreted the existing communist economy, not as a textbook command economy, but as a very imperfect market economy (because it was not possible to suppress human behavior, the spontaneity of exchange, implicit if not explicit prices, bargaining, and the like); with George Stigler we knew that the feasibility of planning is not dependent on the quality and quantity of computers but on the costs of information because information is not a free commodity but an economic asset; with Stigler and Becker we knew that not to be able to specify the role of income and prices in any economic (and noneconomic) issue means that we simply have not looked enough; with Coase we discovered the importance of various forms of transactions costs— in our case especially of search costs in a situation of permanent market disequilibrium.

We have no time and motivation now to put all that in sophisticated articles and books, but I hope there will be time to do so someday.

Such an economic paradigm connected with a special interpretation of the communist economy helped us to organize the transformation of a communist country into a free society and a full-fledged market economy. We had a clear vision of where to go and a pragmatic strategy for getting there. We refused constructivist attempts to organize the transformation as an exercise in applied economics; we accepted the whole process as a delicate mixture of planned and unplanned events, of intentions and spontaneity (see chapter 4); we do not believe in masterminding societal change.

We have definitely crossed the Rubicon and entered the post-transformation stage with a privatized, liberalized, deregulated economy; with a balanced budget, low unemployment and inflation; and with other favorable macroeconomic results. I am sure our success is more than partly the result of the influence of the University of Chicago.

28. Tolerance and Intolerance in Literature and Elsewhere

It is very difficult for a politician to set about writing an essay. In so doing, he consciously or unconsciously casts himself in a certain "nonpolitical" role, but his words—that is, what the politician indicates or directly announces to readers in this form—are still taken as a kind of foreshadowing of "what will be." In our democratic society that kind of reception is not even remotely justified, since our political and constitutional system today is pluralistic, not authoritarian, and a politician really does not announce anything official in an essay. At the same time, it is true that a politician is unable to free his texts of a certain didacticism; he is constantly trying to explain, clarify, persuade, convince, or simply "show." Certainly, the following essay is no exception.

The simplified idea that tolerance means "merely" elevating the virtuous and perhaps indubitable requirement that people be decent and good to each other, and that they respect and honor each other, is indeed correct in principle, but at the same time it is empty and misleading enough to require greater precision or completion. To avoid oversimplification, it may be useful to take a brief look at history and recall when, and in what circumstances, the concept of tolerance first appeared in Europe. It appeared in the 17th century, on the threshold of the Enlightenment, during an era characterized by religious disputes that were never peace loving or "tolerant." Those disputes—not only within individual lands but among lands—very often were violent. The question posed in that period went something like this: How should a state and its institutions act toward individual currents of religious thought and toward the extremely divergent associations of its citizens based on those currents? Until that time, the principle of *cuius regio eius religio* ("he

---

Essay prepared for the world congress of the International Pen Club, Prague, November 1994, and comments made during a panel discussion.

who reigns decides the religion") had led to the unrelieved suffering of those who dared to express their different truths aloud, to wars that dragged on for years, and to the ravishment of entire nations by those in power.

That is just what the Czechs experienced more than once on their own hides, and their memories of it are not the fondest. But thanks to those experiences, they have something to add to the discussion of tolerance.

Calls for tolerance, for a certain spirit of mutual conciliation, were first brought to the table during discussions on relations between the state and the Church in regard to religious confessions, and thus were calls for religious tolerance. The state, whose mission was to make possible and, in a very restricted sense, perhaps even increase the earthly well-being of its citizens (even if we as liberals hold critical views of that function), had no right to influence nonearthly matters, "eternal" questions, affairs concerning the salvation of the human soul. Those matters had to be completely and exclusively within the jurisdiction of the individual alone, of the citizen, who could never relinquish that basic right and never entrust it to any enlightened state institution. Whenever that did happen, the result was devastating—no less in this century than in centuries past.

Because religious belief is only one variant or dimension of an individual's belief system, the secularization of spiritual life that followed caused the concept of tolerance gradually to expand outside the area of religion. The issue then became the tolerance of people (individuals) and the state (and its institutions) for "-isms" of the most diverse sort. Thanks to this, the idea became increasingly accepted, at least in Europe, that the state had no right to intervene in that sphere, neither by giving clear preference to any one set of beliefs (e.g., by raising it to a state ideology) nor by repressing any other beliefs with the means at its disposal, namely its power.

Obviously, the problem is that, for many citizens, to "have" certain convictions or to ponder things is not enough. They want more opportunities and possibilities to proclaim their beliefs publicly and to draw in others for a crack at trying to convince them of the truth. That was more or less universally accepted, and the question became only what kind of limits on individual proclamations of personal truth to impose from outside, for example, how to handle a sect that clearly intended to use its power to the detriment of those who thought differently and thus to interfere with their freedom. Democratic states are still contending with that problem, and the recent rise of extremist political movements, even in those European countries that at first glance seem the most democratic, is more than a mere warning. It is fortunate, and at the same time a great credit to us, that those movements are so far not finding much response here.

If we begin to take a look at the ostensibly trivial concept of tolerance at this more general level, it is clear that in no case does tolerance signify a call for passivity and indifference; nor lead to the demand that opposing views everywhere be suffered quietly; nor ask us to accept views that we find mistaken, deviant, or harmful. The responsibility of a tolerant person is to listen attentively to others and to attempt to understand what they are saying; it is also to consider whether their views, in spite of outward differences, do not speak to oneself as well, to the point perhaps of making one reconsider or even completely revise one's original viewpoint.

Such listening is necessary, but as soon as I come to the conclusion that I understand and that what the other person is saying is incompatible with my convictions or with empirically verifiable evidence, I have not only the right but indeed the responsibility to point out publicly where the error is and to attempt to convince others that I am right. False conciliation must stand aside, because abiding by the principles of human behavior does not mean tolerating errors, untruths, evil, or anything bad. Standing up against those things is the responsibility of us all.

Tolerance is primarily a personal stance, but it is secondarily an institutional affair. The state must guarantee the basic institutional preconditions for the free exchange and confrontation of ideas, which in and of itself can be—and often is—quite sharp. In this institutional view, a special and significant task falls to the underlying democratic institutions that maintain the space for political plurality, especially parliament and a free press. Those institutions must

- enable everyone to express his or her views without external restriction or coercion,
- deny anyone the right to increase his or her freedom at the expense of someone else's,
- ensure that only those ideas receiving the support of a majority of citizens are effectuated by society,

157

- protect the right of minorities to stand by their views and attempt to realize them within the framework of institutionally ensured freedom.

If we apply that point of view, it becomes clear, perhaps a bit surprisingly for some people, that tolerance does not constitute an all-embracing idyll of mutual understanding, acknowledgment, and back patting; it is, rather, a positive way of solving societal conflicts and a rule for communication among people with divergent opinions and antithetical interests, people who often do not get along well with one another on an individual basis.

Without question, tolerance is also built on trust, on trusting that another person can be enlisted for a good cause, and conversely, that no one can be won for long to a cause that is false or condemnable. And it is founded on the assumption that holding faulty or incorrect views constitutes above all an error and not ill will. That broader perspective thus points to something that is both "before" and "above" tolerance, namely the pervasive Judeo-Christian foundations of our civilization.

The world congress of the International Pen Club here in Prague is dedicated to literature rather than to the individual or to societal institutions, and therefore I would like—and I emphasize, as a reader and not a writer of literature—to say a few words about it.

As far as tolerance is concerned, literature is in practice a special case. Artistic works and creations are by nature not such that one work can exclude or deny another even if that were precisely what the author was trying to do and even though certainly nothing like "pure" art exists. The worldview of an artist—whether he wishes it or not—always appears in his work somehow. In this context it would be possible to speak about tolerance only in a very figurative sense of the word, in part because the pleasure a person derives from one specific work of art and the indifference with which he greets another, perhaps even universally recognized, work are quite private matters; and as every artist has proven to himself many times, no kind of outside argument can be of much help.

Art's uniqueness perhaps lies precisely in this nearly unpredictable process, by which individual artworks or entire artistic movements receive or fail to receive universal recognition. Thus no criticism ever is nor can ever be universal recognition. Thus no criticism ever is nor can ever be "pure" criticism, something without value biases. A person—and thus also a literary critic—has a fundamental right to like some things and not others, as well as the right to publicly state the reasons that led him to his conclusions.

Unfortunately, it happens all too often that those reasons remain only an explanation of how and in some cases why a work appeals to him or does not. They contain no kind of objective justification for judging the quality of a work, and a critic can hardly be tolerant toward what does not appeal to him, even if he somehow tries to be. That is precisely what creates problems and "intolerance" in the art world.

Tolerance is here rather an institutional matter—a matter of enabling artists to present themselves to the public and art critics to be heard. Institutionally guaranteeing freedom for both artistic works and artistic criticism is of no small importance. We Czechs in particular had a generally unhappy experience with "state art" during the communist dictatorship, but that experience shows that the problem is pervasive. The most valuable artistic works often arose on the fringes of society, were created over a long period of time in the face of societal indifference, and at the time of their creation had a value known only to a few. Nothing was to be done about it, however, because those works were breakthroughs, and if everyone had suddenly comprehended them, there would have been no breakthrough to discuss.

The Czech essayist and literary critic František Xaver Šalda sometimes became exasperated by the philistine tastes of the political representatives of the First Republic, but that does not seem appropriate to me. Certainly it would have been a fine thing if all politicians had been refined connoisseurs of modern artistic values—except that that requires a certain type of talent that is not necessarily given to everyone. Had they possessed it, it would certainly have been better for them to have become art critics instead of politicians. As long as this or that politician has a sufficient supply of political talent, then the fundamental and most important criterion has been met for him to be able to contribute appropriately to society. In this instance, the lack of an ear for music should be forgiven him. All in all, this is the question of tolerance, in this case of artists for nonartists.

We should therefore take as our starting point the idea that the state is essentially incompetent in matters of culture and art, that any kind of intervention—let me note that intervention means any decision of the commission that distributes state funds earmarked for the arts—can cause more damage than good, and that the state will only charge through this fragile field like a bull in a china shop.

In their works, creators of art are never completely independent (unless they are "creating" only for themselves) for the simple reason that they need money for their work. Ideally, they would be materially dependent only on those to whom their works are directed: readers of their books and those who attend their plays, films, concerts, and exhibitions. That dependence (if dependence can be spoken of at all) is natural because an artist's audience is composed of receivers, of "consumers" of artistic works, and the audience therefore evaluates those works, among other ways, by its willingness to pay for them.

However, many artistic works are by nature directed toward a very tight circle of people, and therefore artists are often unable to depend financially merely on the sale of their work on the market. It is precisely here that the usual fears that artist and art lover have about the commercialization of culture arise, and the word "commercialization" has such a pejorative meaning in this context for just that reason. But let us allow that even "commercial" artworks should come into being.

To enable the creation of other types of artworks, patrons and sponsors—in government as well as in the private sphere—are essential. And finding sponsors is certainly the task of local foundations and other organizations specializing in that activity—again, state as well as private. Let us not place our faith, however, in sponsors or foundations being divinely objective and impartial toward art or artists. They are and always will be institutions run by people, and people will always embrace some artistic position or view of the world. Let us not therefore fall under the illusion that private institutions will be more tolerant of artists and their art than are state institutions, or vice versa. For that reason it is essential that support for artistic activity be ensured by several entities so that the maximum possible diversity exists, enabling artists to compete for support where their art is most in consonance with the tastes, understanding, and perhaps—let's not be afraid of the word—even the interests of potential sponsors.

The state should be only one among many sponsors (and probably not the most important). It seems to me logical and just that taxpayer money be granted by state institutions and money from private sponsors by private institutions. Only a pluralism secured in that way can act as a guarantor of what art is really all about, a guarantor of the freedom of artistic creation. That is one of the consummate expressions of human tolerance.

* * *

Thank you for inviting me to participate in your panel discussion. The topic, "Relations between the Government and Independent Intellectuals," provokes and inspires me. I would like to discuss it from my special perspective as both an intellectual and a government official.

But, as usual, the equation must be properly defined (or formulated)—if not, it has no solution. If we look at the variables of the equation, "government" on the one hand and "independent intellectuals" on the other, there is either one adjective too many or one adjective missing. You have either to eliminate the adjective "independent" or to add the adjective "unfree" (or "totalitarian") to the word "government."

To divide intellectuals into two groups, "independent" and "dependent," has meaning only in a society that is not free. In a democratic country and a free society, that distinction is artificial and meaningless. To call economists (or any other academic professionals) in government institutions "dependent" and economists in research institutes and think tanks "independent" is misleading. Both participate in the formulation and exchange of ideas, and it is their nontransferable task to do that wherever they are employed. The idea (implicit in the title of today's seminar) that the intellectuals who are not associated with government institutions are more objective and more scientifically unbiased is untenable. It is probably even worse. It is dangerous because it suggests or implies that intellectuals should be, a priori, against any government, that they should not communicate with it, that they should remain in their ivory towers and dream about impractical things.

I am, however, convinced that intellectuals are defined, not by their attitude toward government (or the state), but by their ability or inability to formulate ideas; to address other people; to persuade them to think about or to accept their ideas, values, and visions; and to express their thoughts in a coherent and consistent form.

I would accept the term "independent intellectual" in one special sense. It may express and reveal intellectuals' genuine fear of themselves, their fear of misusing their own integrity and role in society and of using the government to promote their ambitious, constructivist ideas and perfectionist projects, so they will be interpreted as "official," instead of using the free market of ideas as their appropriate playground. History knows thousands of cases of the misuse of ideas; history knows the propensity (in economic terminology I would say a very high marginal propensity) of intellectuals for constructivism and social engineering; history knows their tendency to know better than nonintellectuals what is right and what is wrong; history knows their socialist inclinations. Only in that respect may we praise "independent" intellectuals. But it is always better to be a good intellectual than to be an independent one.

My ideas about tolerance are—I hope—sufficiently expressed in my essay, so I will not repeat them now. Tolerance, in my understanding, is not passivity or indifference; it is not an overwhelming, all-embracing love of everybody and everything. Tolerance is the ability to listen, the ability to participate in a dialogue, an openness of mind, and the ability to communicate. It does not require that I accept ideas, attitudes, and deeds of which I disapprove.

29. Review of János Kornai's *The Socialist System: The Political Economy of Communism*

Communism is over, but its legacy influences and will influence the process of transition to a free society as well as the future societal system in our part of the world for some time to come. It is, therefore, relevant to discuss communism's structure, logic, and functioning even if we may hope we are talking about something that definitely belongs to the past. For that reason, we consider János Kornai's book worth discussing.

Previous Discussions of Kornai's Work

The work of János Kornai has been known in the Czech Republic ever since his *Anti-Equilibrium* was published in 1971. His concepts and ideas attracted our attention and provoked reactions; special seminars were held to discuss his approach to economic science and to socialist reality. Questions were raised about why Kornai's work attracted such worldwide interest and why he enjoyed respect and attention in so many countries.

It should be noted from the outset that our view of Kornai was always strongly critical, even when a critique of Kornai could have been interpreted as envy or political opportunism. We used every occasion to explain that our approach to socialist economies differs substantially from Kornai's.[1] Unfortunately, that criticism had little chance of reaching Kornai, whose attention seemed at that time to

---

Cowritten with Dušan Tříska, *Buksz*, Winter 1994.

[1]For our critical analysis, see, for example, T. Ježek and V. Klaus, "Rozpory a dilemata Jánose Kornaie," *Finance a Úvěr* (1987): 134–39; V. Klaus and D. Tříska, "Ekonomie Nicholase Kaldora—nová ekonomie, nebo jiné ambice?" *Politická ekonomie* (1987): 995–1003; D. Tříska, "Consumer under Supply Constraint: Homo Sectans," *European Journal of Political Economy* (1989): 441–58; V. Klaus and D. Tříska, "The Economic Centre: The Restructuring and Equilibrium," *Czechoslovak Economic Digest*, no. 1 (1989): 34–56; and chapter 12 of this book.

be focused on his U.S. audience rather than on the Hungarian, not to mention the Czech, economic community.

Later on, after velvet revolutions in our countries, we had another opportunity to evaluate the usefulness of Kornai's approach when preparing radical transformation strategies for dismantling socialism and creating a standard market economy. That experience gave us additional arguments.

Methodology

The roots of our disagreement can be traced back to what we call "Kornai's methodological extravaganza." He, along with some other "nonconformist" analysts, never accepted the charm and power of standard economics.[2] Since he questioned its usefulness even within a market economy, it can be no surprise that he found it fully irrelevant for socialist economies. He adopted his own, nonstandard approach and with its help has sought to produce a value-free, truly objective, that is, positive, analysis.

Nothing can be more remote from our own views than that. Unlike Kornai, we stressed that regardless of how far the reality of socialist economies seems to be from the Arrow-Debreu ideal of perfect competition, they should be treated analytically as any other economy. Also, it was our thesis that there is no positive (value-free) approach to any economy except an approach based on standard economic analysis.

In standard economics, a system under study is always defined by its equilibrium and by fluctuations around it. At the same time, it is understood that the equilibrium may be more or less efficient. Therefore, a system can be extremely inefficient and still be in equilibrium. *Anti-Equilibrium* might have made a nice title for a book, but it has never had any meaning or analytical importance to us.

We did not find justification for innovative tools, but we did find insufficiently defined analytical tools such as "shortage." In addressing demand for goods in "short supply," we have to use such standard (and instrumental) terms as "search function" and "transactions costs."

---

[2]By "standard economics" we understand, in particular, models that have their roots in the so-called neoclassical economic synthesis.

In our own writings we described socialist economies as consisting of firms and households maximizing their utility functions subject to corresponding hard constraints. In our view, it is by definition that a constraint is hard, not soft; the idea of a soft budget has by definition no meaning, and it only demonstrates that the real hard constraint has not been found (or analytically defined).

Vertical relationships are of importance in all economic systems, more in socialist ones than in a standard market economy, and we paid attention to them. However, our analysis always started with horizontal interactions among firms and households, even in socialist economies.

We cannot hide the fact that we never accepted Kornai's creative methodology. His capacity to coin new terms, we admit, made his books accessible to a broad range of readers. On the other hand, his approach could never provide a profound understanding of real-world socialism, and it may even have confused some politicians who have recently attempted to transform their postsocialist countries.

Political System

In *The Socialist System*, Kornai extends his traditional focus and seeks to deal with some political aspects of socialism. That extension does not change our basic evaluation. Even in this field we cannot accept his approach and were not able to appreciate its usefulness. In other words, we never thought it necessary to analyze the communist power structure as an entirely "different animal" and to introduce specific analytical tools in order to analyze it. On the contrary, we extended the standard paradigm of economics beyond economies and applied it to the behavior of political agents (the approach of the public-choice school of thought was our inspiration). Unlike Kornai, we agreed that political systems can be described by costs and benefits, individual utilities, optimization, overall welfare, and equilibrium.

Keeping political science value free is most difficult. Unfortunately, Kornai, who formally refuses normativism, in this nonstandard "political economy of communism," makes numerous value-loaded accusations of communism. While he has no mercy for communists, he provides no comprehensive and feasible scheme for getting rid of them.

165

In our view, communists had (and in the Czech Republic still have) a party that is more or less like any other: it fights for political power and, once seized, seeks to keep it. To make its life easier, the party attempts to establish itself as a monopoly.

The communist party behaves not only like any other political party but also like any business firm that attempts to prevent further entries of potential competitors. The positive (standard-type) approach of economics has the capacity to analyze the relative efficiency of a monopolistic (totalitarian) structure as compared with a competitive (democratic) one. However clear this problem may be ideologically, a serious efficiency analysis is far from trivial and, unfortunately, no help is offered by Kornai.

Economics of Transformation

As already indicated, different methodologies (and interpretations of socialist economies) give rise to different concepts of the subject matter of transformation. In drafting our transformation strategy, we assumed that a socialist economy can and should be defined in terms of specific market imperfections and distortions. Clearly, then, the true objective of the transformation process could not be dismantling central planning, and it definitely could not be "establishing" a market economy, since a market economy, however imperfect, already existed. Each alternative transformation strategy consists of external, government-organized measures to which the economy under transformation is to be subjected. Doubtless, not every imaginable strategy need be realizable; a set of feasible strategies must be, therefore, defined. The notion of feasibility especially reflects the facts that transformation has its own (inherent) dynamics and that the government operates only within a well-defined "transformation possibilities frontier." Put differently, there are also in action other external and internal forces, most important of which is the behavior of millions of participants—citizens of the respective countries.

Unfortunately, little can be found in Kornai's book about various extremely practical issues raised by the transformation challenge. Quite a lot—we are convinced—may be learned here from standard economic textbooks.

Returning to our methodological observations, economics shows why transition from one equilibrium to another is difficult.

Speed and Timing

The economics of transformation, as a truly positive approach to postsocialist realty, produces surprisingly strong practical recommendations. For purposes of demonstration, it may be of value to present three of the most fundamental principles of the Czech transformation strategy, since none of them finds room in Kornai's book.

Our strategy for transforming the political system was indirect in the sense that it included no direct measures against the Communist Party. (The issue of the party's future legality was, of course, raised in the Czech Republic.) The government solved the problem indirectly: the political environment was liberalized, that is, free entry was secured for newly emerging political groups. As a result, a basically unreformed communist party remained in Parliament, though in opposition. (In some other postsocialist countries, what we would call "direct" strategies were adopted, and, as a result, the reformed communists control their respective parliaments now.)

The transformation strategy for state-owned enterprises was direct, firm, and transparent. The Czech government had no doubt that without government-organized mass privatization, the newly emerging private businesses would be too vulnerable to the monopolistic practices of the rent-seeking state-owned enterprises.

Speed was regarded as absolutely essential to successful transformation, and, therefore, no strategy was regarded as feasible unless it was capable of producing results fast. In economic terms, the benefits of gradualism may be appreciated only by those who disregard the costs of transformation.

Unfortunately, even though most of Kornai's book is devoted to "shifting from communism," almost nothing is said about speed and timing or about what we believe are the absolutely crucial ingredients of an optimal transformation strategy.

Comparative Economic Systems

The approach that treats a socialist economy as any other economy, of course, does not neglect thousands of distinctions among different economies. Standard economics has devoted a lot of effort to proper identification of the differences and similarities among various economies, and it has sought to classify economies accordingly.

It may be of value to respond to Kornai's comparison of the transformability of Hungary and the Czech Republic. He believes that the former country will complete its transformation with greater ease precisely because it started its reforms long before the latter one. On page 460, Kornai states, ". . . the greater the extent to which both the formal and informal private sector has managed to develop . . . the faster the advance of the private sector will be after the change of system." That and some other similar observations, in our view, to a great degree incorporate the error of Kornai's approach to socialism. Therefore, two comments may be in order.

First, the economic reforms observed in Hungary in the 1970s and 1980s (and designed in Czechoslovakia in the 1960s) should never be conceived of as an efficient economic change (in whatever sense of the term). Second, the institutional outcomes of perestroika-type reforms necessarily complicate the genuine transformation of an economy.

We have to admit that we have never supported implementation of Hungarian-style economic reform, and it seems to us that the results of transformation to date prove that we were right. This brings us, again, to our arguments about speed, the factor almost totally neglected by Kornai. In transforming an economy, every month and every week matters. If the government-organized measures come late, however hard and well targeted they may be, they will have no effect because their timing is wrong. Falling even one day behind the original timetable may destroy the whole strategy.

Concluding Statement

We do not want to discuss details, but some are worth mentioning. On page 460 the author says, "Inevitably, it will take many years before the private sector becomes the dominant sphere in the economy." On page 512 he continues, "The old party-state was unable to induce real market behavior in state-owned firms. The new democratic system must show that it really can be done. . . . I cannot refrain from expressing doubts about the reality of it."

Both quotations demonstrate Kornai's lack of ability to understand what is going on in our part of the world and even in his native country. The question, "What should be done with the remaining state-owned enterprises?" may have some meaning only in perestroika, not in a fundamental systemic change. The government has just one option—privatize the enterprises fast and never ask questions about their restructuring or corporate governance. If the government wants to help, it should focus on promoting the growth of new private businesses.

On pages 527–28, Kornai issues the following warning about gradual versus full-fledged price liberalization: "Careful observation and comparative analysis of future experiences will reveal what advantages and drawbacks are attached to applying one or other of these alternative policies."

Economists know that price regulation and consequent gradual deregulation undermine what the economy needs most—stability. Both the transformed and the newly emerged economic agents have enough uncertainties to face—the legal framework is changing, tax reforms are developing, accountancy rules are emerging, traditional (Eastern) markets are shrinking, and Western competitors are expanding their market shares. Kornai seems to be totally unaware of the impact of gradual deregulation. Any price deregulation has the capacity to convert profit makers into loss makers and vice versa. Gradual deregulation is a sin and—if committed—it should be justified in a different (e.g., noneconomic) way than can be found in Kornai's book.

Kornai is concerned about upward pressure on wages, the investment sector, state budget deficits, increases in the money supply, inflation, and unemployment. The point he wants to stress on page 564 is that ". . . the classical system, with its repression and bureaucratic constraints, is better able to resist a high proportion of these tendencies than the half-relaxed, half-regressive reform system. Precisely because the administration of the state will be in the hands of democratic governments in the future, there is a danger that they will be unable to resist . . . the negative tendencies. . . ."

Here we blame Kornai for the excuse he makes for himself when he states that he "only draws attention to the likely problems and dangers." Perhaps it would be too much to ask a pure scientist for solutions to real-world problems. However, it is perfectly fair to expect from him a cause-and-effect analysis such as "if the government adopts policy X, then there is an n percent probability that Y will happen and Z will get beyond control."

Who else, if not the renowned experts on socialism, should be capable of producing those types of forecasts? Whose job and responsibility is it, if not Kornai's?

Selected Bibliography of Works by Václav Klaus

Between the Past and the Future (in Czech). Brno: Universitas Masarykiana Foundation, 1996.

The Czech Way (in Czech). Prague: Profile, 1994.

Dismantling Socialism: A Road to Market Economy II (in English). Prague: Top Agency, 1992.

Economic Theory and Economic Reform (in Czech). Prague: Gennex and Top Agency, 1991.

Economic Theory and Reality of Transformation Processes (in Czech). Prague: Management Press, 1995.

I Do Not Like Catastrophic Scenarios (in Czech). Ostrava: Sagit, 1991.

Karel Hvížď'ala: The First on the Right Side (in Czech). Interview with Václav Klaus. Prague: Cartonia, 1992.

Rebirth of a Country: Five Years After (in English). Prague: Ringier, 1994.

A Road to Market Economy (in English). Prague: Top Agency, 1991.

Signale aus dem Herzen Europas (in German). Gabler: Gennex, 1991.

Summing Up to One (in Czech). Prague: Management Press, Ringier, 1995.

Tomorrow's Challenge (in Czech). Prague: Pražská Imaginace, 1991.

Tschechische Transformation und Europäische Integration: Gemeinsamkeiten von Visionen und Strategien (in German). Passau: Neue Press, 1995.

Why Am I a Conservative? (in Czech). Prague: Top Agency, 1992.

The Year—How Much Is It in the History of the Country? (in Czech). Vienna: Compress, 1993.

Index

About the Author

Václav Klaus was born in 1941 in Prague. In 1963 he graduated from the Prague School of Economics where he studied international economic relations and international trade. He studied economics in Italy in 1966 and at Cornell University in 1969. Until 1970 he worked as a researcher in the Institute of Economics of the Czechoslovak Academy of Sciences. His main areas of interest were macroeconomic theory, monetary and fiscal policies, and comparative economics.

After the invasion of Czechoslovakia by Warsaw Pact forces in 1968, Klaus was forced to leave the Academy of Sciences for political reasons, and from 1971 to 1986 he occupied various lower level positions in the Czechoslovak State Bank. In 1987 he was allowed to return to the Academy of Sciences and became head of the Department for Macroeconomic Policy in the newly formed Institute of Forecasting.

Klaus was one of the founders of the Czechoslovak Civic Forum, and in October 1990 he was elected its chairman. In February 1991 the Civic Forum split into two factions, one of which constituted itself into the Civic Democratic Party. Klaus was elected chairman of that party at the founding congress in April 1991.

He was the first noncommunist finance minister appointed after more than 40 years of communist rule. In October 1991 he became deputy prime minister of Czechslovakia, and in June 1992, after a Civic Forum victory in the parliamentary elections, he was appointed prime minister of the Czech Republic.

Klaus is a member of the Mont Pèlerin Society and a fellow of the Adam Smith Institute in London and the Centro de Estudios Publicos in Santiago de Chile. He has received numerous international awards and honorary doctorates from institutions of higher learning. His writings on inflation, monetary and fiscal policy, comparative economic systems, and economic transformation have been published in both scholarly and popular journals.

Cato Institute

Founded in 1977, the Cato Institute is a public policy research foundation dedicated to broadening the parameters of policy debate to allow consideration of more options that are consistent with the traditional American principles of limited government, individual liberty, and peace. To that end, the Institute strives to achieve greater involvement of the intelligent, concerned lay public in questions of policy and the proper role of government.

The Institute is named for *Cato's Letters*, libertarian pamphlets that were widely read in the American Colonies in the early 18th century and played a major role in laying the philosophical foundation for the American Revolution.

Despite the achievement of the nation's Founders, today virtually no aspect of life is free from government encroachment. A pervasive intolerance for individual rights is shown by government's arbitrary intrusions into private economic transactions and its disregard for civil liberties.

To counter that trend, the Cato Institute undertakes an extensive publications program that addresses the complete spectrum of policy issues. Books, monographs, and shorter studies are commissioned to examine the federal budget, Social Security, regulation, military spending, international trade, and myriad other issues. Major policy conferences are held throughout the year, from which papers are published thrice yearly in the *Cato Journal*. The Institute also publishes the quarterly magazine *Regulation*.

In order to maintain its independence, the Cato Institute accepts no government funding. Contributions are received from foundations, corporations, and individuals, and other revenue is generated from the sale of publications. The Institute is a nonprofit, tax-exempt, educational foundation under Section 501(c)3 of the Internal Revenue Code.

CATO INSTITUTE
1000 Massachusetts Ave., N.W.
Washington, D.C. 20001